08.

08.

SPECIAL OPERATIONS in IRAQ

SPECIAL OPERATIONS in IRAQ

MIKE RYAN

Pen & Sword

MILITARY

First published in Great Britain in 2004 by
Pen & Sword Military
an imprint of
Pen & Sword Books Ltd
47 Church Street
Barnsley
South Yorkshire
S70 2AS

Copyright © Mike Ryan 2004
ISBN 1 84415 032 1

A CIP catalogue record for this book is
available from the British Library

For a complete list of Pen & Sword titles please contact
PEN & SWORD BOOKS LIMITED
47 Church Street, Barnsley, South Yorkshire, S70 2AS, England
E-mail: enquiries@pen-and-sword.co.uk
Website: www.pen-and-sword.co.uk

CONTENTS

PREFACE

On 20 March 2003 America and her coalition allies, Britain, Australia and Poland, began a war with Iraq that would eventually culminate in the fall of its evil leader, Saddam Hussein, and his much feared Ba'ath party regime.

Although much has already been written about this war, the full story has yet to be told. What has been written in recent months only covers the overt, conventional military operations that took place during the conflict, as these were the only actions that the world's media was ever invited to cover. However, there was another war taking place at the same time. It was being fought in the shadows of Iraq, far from the attention of the media and, therefore, far from the attention of the public, as that is the preferred modus operandi of a very special group of individuals. They are, of course, the operators of the Special Forces; a group of men, and sometimes even women, who fought a very personal war around the barren and desolate battlefields of Iraq, during what became known as Operation Iraqi Freedom. Their exploits, for the most part, were unseen, unheard and unsung. Only now can their covert and highly secret war be revealed.

DEDICATION

This book is dedicated to the brave and selfless members of the British, American, Australian and Polish Special Forces who served their countries so well during Operation Iraqi Freedom.

Their courage and professionalism is an inspiration to us all.

ACKNOWLEDGEMENTS

I would like to thank the following individuals, organizations and companies for their kind help, for without them there could be no book.

Brigadier Henry Wilson, Jon Wilkinson for the great book cover, Major M., Colonel Petraeus, Colonel S., Major I., 'Ginga', 'Oz', Mr T., Rob, Big D, USAF PA, SOCOM, PA the White House, US Navy, 160th SOAR, 75th Ranger Regiment, 101st Airborne Division (Air Assault), 16 Air Assault Brigade, UK MOD, US DoD, 4 RAR, SASR, Royal Marines, 131 CDO, Australian DoD, DVIC, NARA, USMC and last, but certainly not least, Avpro Aerospace.

All photographs, unless otherwise stated, are courtesy of the UK MOD, US DoD, Australian DoD, DVIC and the US Navy.

Finally, as always, a special thanks to my wife Fiona and my daughters, Isabella and Angelina, for their kind support during the time I spent researching and writing this book.

AUTHOR'S NOTE

Due to ongoing military operations in Iraq, certain technical, tactical and procedural details have had to be either changed or omitted to comply with both UK and US operational security (OPSEC) requirements. I make no apology for this as the safety of both our military personnel, and those of our allies, is paramount.

INTRODUCTION

On 19 March, 2003, President George W. Bush gave Saddam Hussein a warning: leave Iraq within forty-eight hours or else face the consequences.

Anticipating that Saddam would defy him and hold a council of war with his fellow Ba'ath party members as a response, President Bush gave the go-ahead for a pre-emptive 'decapitation attack', the idea being to terminate the top Iraqi leadership in one precise surgical strike, thereby negating the need for a war. The decision was certainly a gamble, as it altered months of meticulous military planning that had been in place since November 2002 - the original preferred date for a war against Iraq. But, nonetheless, it was a risk deemed worthy of taking, as it would save lives, both friendly and enemy alike, assuming of course that Saddam was going to be in the location that was about to be targeted.

President Bush however, was not acting on a hunch or, indeed, a piece of satellite imagery to justify his confidence; he was acting on a good, old fashioned, solid but extremely reliable, intelligence tip-off provided by a Mk 1 eyeball on the ground, its owner being a member of the CIA's super secret Special Operations Group (SOG). This unit, although largely unknown prior to Operation Iraqi Freedom, had a good reputation for getting its hands dirty quickly in times of tension and hostility and had had boots on the ground in Baghdad, operating covertly for many months prior to the outbreak of hostilities with Iraq, its role being to gather intelligence and encourage insurrection.

Within military circles, such an operation is referred to as a 'stake through the heart' mission, as its effects can be awesome if successful, but disastrous if poorly planned and executed; a classic example being Operation Market during the Second World War.

On 20 March 2003, at approximately 05.30 hours local time (02.30 GMT), cruise missiles, launched from ships and submarines deployed in and around the Gulf region, began impacting on the city of Baghdad in a spectacular manner. As impressive as it first appeared to be, this was not an attack on the scale originally billed as forming part of the much heralded 'Shock and Awe' campaign, which boasted of hitting Iraq with an initial strike of some 3,000 cruise missiles.

By early morning as the smoke wafted across the city of Baghdad from the carcass of the building that was supposed to be Saddam's tomb, word quickly spread throughout the streets, tea shops and bazaars that Saddam had been mortally wounded in the precision strike the night before, as his personal ambulance had been spotted arriving at the scene of the attack shortly after the missiles had stopped falling. This, however, proved to be a case of wishful thinking, as sources later confirmed that he had survived the attack and was now in hiding; place or places unknown.

As President Bush contemplated this news, coalition ground forces from the United States, United Kingdom, Australia and Poland began invading Iraq by means of land, sea and air. However, there was one group of individuals whose war had begun long before this. It was, of course, the covert war fought by those of the Special Forces. It is now known that some elements of the British SAS entered Iraq, via Jordan in August 2002, some eight months prior to the official commencement of hostilities. Their mission was to watch MSRs (Main Supply Routes) for troop movements and to gather intelligence on possible targets. For cover they passed themselves off as oil smugglers and drove around in battered old fuel tankers that had been hollowed out to allow the carriage of both personnel and equipment. It proved to be a good ruse as the Iraqis turned a blind eye to oil smugglers, especially if they paid good bribes. During their time in Iraq, the SAS were able to link up with various agencies operating in the region, such as MI6, the CIA and, of course, 'Gray Fox', the US Army's covert intelligence arm. At times, there appeared to be more agents from overseas operating in Iraq, than there were Iraqi agents. Although many of them were in Iraq for military intelligence gathering purposes, most were there to find evidence of Iraq's Weapons of Mass Destruction (WMD) programme, as this was the official premise for going to war with Iraq.

For the Special Forces, there was much work to be done in Iraq prior to the coalition forces military campaign. Operations carried out included:

Tactical reconnaissance
Strategic reconnaissance
Close Target Reconnaissance
Target Identification
Reconnaissance of routes of ingress
Reconnaissance of routes of egress
Troop Observations
Reconnaissance of military road traffic movement
Identification of friendly indigenous forces
Identification of hostile enemy forces (both conventional and unconventional).
Sabotage of communications systems and networks
Sabotage of transportation systems
Reconnaissance of beaches and landing points.
Reconnaissance of bridges and lines of communication
Reconnaissance of defended positions (including minefields)

and finally, probably the most important mission of all, the reconnaissance of suspected WMD research sites.

To accomplish such a complex task required massive Special Forces resources, both from the UK and the USA and, bearing in mind that ongoing counter-terrorist operations post 9-11 were still taking place in Afghanistan, Yemen, Somalia and the Philippines , this was no easy task.

THE DIFFERENCE BETWEEN THE TWO GULF WARS

One of the most extraordinary military campaigns ever conducted, was how US Vice President Richard Cheney described Operation Iraqi Freedom when giving brief details of what led to success in Iraq.

The campaign that US and coalition forces launched on 19 March followed 'a carefully drawn plan with fixed objectives and the flexibility to meet them,' he said in a speech to the US Heritage Foundation in Washington.

It would be very easy to write off Operation Iraqi Freedom as an extended version of Desert Storm, but that would not be the case. There are some similarities, but there are also great differences, especially when it comes to Special Forces. In the first Gulf War, Special Forces were viewed as a sideline act, whereas in Iraqi Freedom they were the main event, only you didn't get to hear too much about their activities. For a start we had the good old Scud hunting teams and the road watch teams; the same MO as Desert Storm but different players.

Operation Desert Storm 1991. A burnt out Iraqi tank stands half buried in the desert after a direct hit from an Allied aircraft.

Secondly, there were the intensive tactical reconnaissance and targeting missions that proved critical to the success of Operation Iraqi Freedom, as they greatly increased operational efficiency and effectiveness thus minimizing collateral damage.

And finally, we have the Special Forces support operations that were designed to encourage insurrection and to reduce Saddam's military forces and their will to fight. By all accounts these missions went to plan but the enemy resistance experienced, was greater than originally anticipated, especially in the case of post war Iraq.

In the case of military hardware, most of the weaponry used in the recent conflict was the same as that used in 1991, only the efficiency and targeting of it was vastly greater, especially in the case of precision guided munitions (PGMs).

Operation Iraqi Freedom also saw the deployment of low risk munitions such as the cement bomb, an air-dropped weapon that is designed for use in built-up urban areas where there is a high risk of collateral damage; its preferred method of targeting being courtesy of Special Forces operatives. In one well documented incident, a British SAS

Operation Iraqi Freedom 2003. Twelve years on, an Iraqi tank suffers the same fate after fierce fighting with the Royal Marines outside Basra.

Crated boxes of ammunition are prepared for an airlift prior to the Al Faw operation.

soldier targeted an Iraqi tank located near to a school and requested that it be knocked out by means of a cement bomb, or a Blue Circle as the SAS would say. The RAF, keen to oblige, dropped the first cement bomb but it failed to destroy the tank, prompting the SAS soldier to say *'That was real impressive, but next time can we have one that goes bang please.'*

Not all technology deployed in Operation Iraqi Freedom worked to plan, despite the best intentions of its user. But one thing that did work well was the operatives themselves. In a deployment that was truly massive in terms of its size and scope, Special Forces played a critical role in every dimension of this war, especially in southern, western and northern Iraq, where their presence was most keenly felt.

Essentially, the Australians operated primarily in western Iraq but had elements of their forces in central and southern locations. The Americans, on the other hand, operated throughout Iraq but were particularly strong in the southern, central and northern areas of the country whereas the British operated very strongly in the south, north and western regions of Iraq. Last, but by no means least, the Polish, operated solely in the south of Iraq, primarily around the port of Umm Qasr, on the Al Faw peninsula.

THE ROLE OF SPECIAL FORCES IN OPERATION IRAQI FREEDOM

The largest US Special Operations force since the Vietnam War was supporting the war in Iraq. While the vast majority of Special Operations forces are American, the UK and Australia are also providing *'very capable forces,'* said Major General Stanley McChrystal, vice chief of operations on the US Joint Staff, on 4 April.

'Special Operations forces are more extensive in this campaign than any I've seen. Probably as a percentage effort, they are unprecedented for a war that also has a conventional part to it.'

He said that in northern Iraq there was a significant Special Operations presence. Coalition personnel were working with Kurdish fighters against the regime. Special Operations personnel were helping achieve stability in the area.

'They helped bring in the 173rd Airborne Brigade last week, and they are marking and calling in coalition air power on regime targets. In the west, there is a large area denial mission, which is very, very effective at this point,' the Major General stated.

Special Operations forces were also responsible for attacking a number of specific targets, such as airfields, weapons of mass destruction sites and command and control headquarters.

Polish GROM operators and US Navy Seals, assist each other in taking Iraqi POWs into custody.

He said that in the south, Special Operations personnel gave aid to conventional forces and did some of the work in the cities to help the Shi'ia elements.

When the campaign began, US Dept of Defense officials said 'hundreds' of Special Operations forces were in Iraq. Two weeks into the war, that number had risen.

CHAPTER ONE

SPECIAL & ELITE FORCES AT WAR

ACCOUNT FROM AUSTRALIAN SASR OPERATIVE

'In all there were around 80 of us operating in western Iraq, but to the Iraqis it must have seemed like 800. Our primary role was to stop weapons of mass destruction from being launched from the 1991 'Scud Line' in the western Iraqi desert, while our secondary role was to raise merry hell - 'Digger Style'. Basically we were like an enormous itch that the Iraqis could not scratch, as we were everywhere and anywhere. One day we were in the desert, the next in a giant cement works - in this case the one at Kubaysah, about 60 km north of Highway One between Baghdad and Amman and 20 km south of the huge Al Asad air base. This massive civilian infrastructure was nicknamed by us 'The Temple of Doom', and was captured without us firing a single shot - and with 40 prisoners as well.

'However it was not always like this for us, as in several contacts we engaged enemy forces on an ongoing basis for a number of days- fighting running battles with them that were as good as any I experienced in Afghanistan. Along the way we even treated wounded enemy, fed and watered prisoners and then sent them home with a simple message: "The war is over for you."

'During our 42 day incursion, we took on more than 2,000 Iraqis, including elite Republican Guard troops and counter Special Forces troops- although not at the same time-and suffered no casualties-that's got to be a ripper result.

'During our mission we found no Scuds, but we left our own calling card - 46,000 kg of bombs and missiles in the first week of combat alone to be exact. The overwhelming success of the SAS mission to deny the enemy any ballistic missile launches was due to technology, training and superior communications basically. The fact that the squadron suffered no casualties did not surprise me, as we minimized the risks to our own people and to the Iraqis. Despite the lack of casualties and the string of victories, this was no picnic-as the Iraqis were well organized and well equipped. It was one-on-one and it was tough.

'The first SAS patrol to cross into Iraq by night spent 96 hours in open desert terrain without being spotted by anyone, including local Bedouin herdsmen and enemy forces. For them not to get compromised in that dead flat terrain was a significant effort. Although we never saw any Scuds during our deployment, the fact that we were operating as if they were there made a real difference- as the Iraqis

An Australian SAS Perentie shows off its formidable armament while on Patrol.

50·874

15

were always trying to second guess us. It is called manoeuvre warfare and is designed to put pressure on the enemy and to unmask them. We were a small force element creating quite a disproportionate effect - by means of shock and surprise. Also we were completely unpredictable in our actions which were the key components of our tactics. We also had to deal with an unpredictable enemy, who

Surface to Surface missiles posed a great threat to coalition forces throughout Operation Iraqi Freedom, hence the priority of destroying them.

would on occasions raise his hands in surrender yet resume firing as we approached. We even have one of their flags that bears proof of this as it has both powder burns and bullet holes from being fired through. Adding to our operational experience we also had the weather to contend with, as temperatures often ranged from -5C to 43C - and we thought Oz varied. All in all it was a magnificent effort, and a ripper achievement.'

THE AUSTRALIAN SPECIAL FORCES TASK GROUP

Australian forces were not mentioned very much by the world's media during the conflict with Iraq, as they seemed to focus on the activities of the British and American forces only. This biased reporting belies the fact that Australian forces did play a significant part in this war, and their efforts need to be recognized by all.

This is an account of Australian Special Forces activities during the war with Iraq, as performed under the umbrella of Operation Falconer. The main element of the Special Forces Task Group deployed to the Middle East in mid-February under the auspices of Operation Bastille, their aim being to acclimatize and prepare for possible roles in the war against Iraq.

At the same time, an Australian Special Operations Forward Command element set up in theatre to command all Special Forces operations in the Middle East. The Special Forces Task Group was manned by personnel from Headquarters Special Operations, the Special Air Service Regiment in Perth, 4 RAR Commando, the Logistics Support Force, the Incident Response Regiment, the 5th Aviation Regiment, plus support personnel from the Army and the RAAF (Royal Australian Air Force), while the SF Headquarters was part of a clearly defined command chain which ensured that Australian Special Forces were always commanded by Australians.

The Headquarters not only commanded the Special Forces Task Group, but provided an important command link to Headquarters Australian Theatre in Sydney and the Australian National Command Headquarters. It was also linked closely to the equivalent Special Operations Command element for the United States and was co-located. This was critical to ensure a full observation and transparency of coalition Special Forces activities and, from all reports, the relationship worked exceptionally well.

By early February 2003, coalition planning had evolved to give a clearly understood role for the Australian Special Forces during Operation Falconer. In accordance with clear government guidance, it was agreed that if there was an eventual Australian commitment, the Task Group was to conduct special operations in western Iraq as part of a coalition effort to defeat the weapons of mass destruction threat. Specifically, their job was to deny Iraq the ability to launch theatre ballistic missiles in the west. Other missions included harassing operations, destruction of critical command and control nodes and operations to prevent the freedom of movement of the Iraqis in the theatre.

A Special Operations Commander discusses the SAS Regiment's objectives before being deployed to Iraq.

When the main contingent first arrived in the Middle East in early February, it started training on the premise that it was likely to be committed; to think otherwise would certainly have risked failure. Consequently, the Task Group conducted what is known as Full Mission Profile Exercises by day and night, stepping through the full range of contingencies that it could expect, if committed to Iraq. This intensive, realistic training period enabled the soldiers to acclimatize in the environmental conditions that they might expect and to hone their skills. This acclimatization and work-up period proved to be of immense value in the war that followed, as Australian Special Forces had to inter-operate regularly with other Special Forces units such as those of the British SAS and the US Delta Force. In relation to air operations this was critical, as the Australians relied heavily upon British and American close air support and any doubt or confusion about

Soldiers attempt to errect a camouflage shelter whilst enduring a desert sandstorm.

location is a recipe for disaster, especially on today's fast-moving battlefield where the possibility of friendly fire incidents are only ever seconds away.

While the acclimatization training was taking place, the task group established a logistic support infrastructure to support the forces once deployed on operations. Known as the Combat Service Support Group, this group consisted of seventy-seven people drawn from nine different regular Australian army units. It had the pivotal role of providing communications support, ordering stores, warehousing, managing freight distribution and providing re-supply, which was normally by air. They also had the job of servicing the wide range of vehicles used by the Special Air Service Regiment, which was no easy task at the best of times but during a sandstorm, where winds could gust at anything up to fifty kilometres per hour, that was something else. Indeed, it was not uncommon for tents to be blown away, leaving equipment, food and personnel exposed to sand and fine dust. On the plus side however, communications and computer networks held up well under the same conditions.

On the transport side, Australian CH-47 Chinooks provided critical combat service support in the rear areas, to free both US and UK aircraft for combat tasks where the pilot's vision is virtually always totally obscured during landings because of the perpetual sand and dust that is everywhere in Iraq.

One of Australia's key assets during this war was the TIRR (The Incident Response Regiment) which was co-located with the Commando Alert Force, its

Australian Chinooks fly over enemy territory at low level to avoid Manpads and SAMs.

Troopers from 4 RAR carry out a sweep of an abandoned Iraqi position in Western Iraq.

task being to deploy into Iraq at short notice to assist in the detection of weapons of mass destruction associated with materials that may have been discovered by the SAS. All personnel operating within the TIRR are highly skilled in their art, as their role is extremely dangerous and demanding. On one occasion during Operation Falconer, they deployed to a giant military complex at Al Asad to conduct a search mission. This was to be a demanding task for them, as the facility was covered with abandoned buildings, bunkers and massive amounts of military hardware, all requiring meticulous attention. After several days of hard searching it was declared safe of weapons of mass destruction as nothing incriminating was found there. Although somewhat

An Australian operator shows off a small cache of ammunition captured at Al Asad.

disappointed at first with this result, the fact that the Task Group could undertake this sort of mission without relying on coalition support, was a major boost to their confidence and clearly justified the robust stand-alone capability that Australia had deployed to this region.

Within the Task Group, the Commando element was regarded as the cavalry of the Australian forces; always ready and willing to be deployed at a moment's notice should anyone need it. To achieve this they established an alert force capability which could be reacted in the event of an emergency, such as that of a downed aircrew. However it could equally be used for the recovery of wounded personnel or to provide assistance to threatened SAS patrols. The alert force also included helicopter assets, medical support and the Incident Response Regiment detachment. It was reassuring for the SAS to know that if they got into trouble they had an alert force manned by the commandos, all Australians of course, who could come in and support them. While the alert force was never activated in anger, the commandos were tasked, towards the end of the campaign, with assisting the SAS in clearing the large Al Asad Air base, securing the Australian mission in Baghdad and providing further support for the medical teams involved with Operation Baghdad Assist.

For most Australian Special Forces operating in Iraq, the western desert was their primary area of operation, an inhospitable place, that's open and bare with few places to hide. This, alone, makes daylight movement almost impossible as the detection risk is just too great because of the Bedouins and local Iraqis.

Just like the British SAS in Desert Storm, the SAS Task Group experienced all

An Australian operator guards a captured Iraqi fighter on the giant Al Asad airbase in western Iraq, whilst his colleague carries out a close inspection for booby-traps.

the extremes that a desert can offer. Early in the conflict the temperatures dropped to minus five degrees, and that's not taking into account the wind chill factor while, later in the war, temperatures exceeded forty degrees Celsius. On one occasion sandstorms blew constantly for two days with winds averaging thirty kilometres an hour, reducing visibility to ten metres. On another occasion, it rained so heavily that the Task Group's weapons' systems were being clogged and jammed by wind blown mud.

Essentially, SAS operations comprised four elements -

THE INSERTION PHASE
THE COMBAT PHASE
THE INTERDICTION PHASE
THE SECURITY PHASE

Firstly the insertion. This, in itself, was quite an achievement. The force inserted by night by vehicle and helicopter into areas remote from friendly conventional forces. The intent was to insert clandestinely and get deep into the assigned area before the sun came up. The vehicle insertion involved breaching an earth berm and trench system and negotiating a network of Iraqi guard posts undetected. This was achieved successfully. However thirty kilometres inside Iraq the force bumped into a number of enemy vehicles. These were engaged by fire and then detained. As they later found out, this was one of the first contacts of the war and one in which SAS medics rendered first-aid to a couple of wounded Iraqi soldiers.

Due to the need to continue the mission, the enemy were released and the force moved on, arriving where they planned to be just on first light without further mishap.

Helicopters played a key role in Special Forces operations in Iraq, but the difficulty and risk of their usage under certain conditions should not be underestimated. In one mission US helicopter forces carrying Australian SAS

The Iraqi Imperial Guard still loyal to Saddam, dig in and prepare to meet the Allied Forces, outside Baghdad.

The difficult and dangerous process of refuelling a helicopter in mid-flight, an operation often conducted by night whilst inserting SAS operatives.

Australian troops patrolling the desert at night using Night Vision goggles .

operatives flew, by night and in poor weather, over 600 kilometres from the SAS staging base deep into Iraq. During the flight, they had to conduct a difficult air-to-air refuelling activity, as well as negotiate an extensive enemy air defence system. After landing they were, at that time, the closest coalition ground elements to Baghdad and they remained that way for a number of days.

The troops may have thought the insertion was demanding and exhilarating, but there was a lot more to come and what followed certainly set the tone for the campaign. The intention of the commander on the ground was not to sit back and wait for the enemy to come to him, or wait for him to deploy his Scud missiles. Rather, he undertook to commit to aggressive operations to unmask the enemy in terms of his intent, his location and his strength. This involved high tempo offensive patrolling in a controlled sequence across the area of operations. At the same time, he needed to maintain a static surveillance on the main access roads down which the enemy could deploy his Scuds or the main larger conventional reaction forces.

This phase coincided with an exceptionally heavy period of activity in the first week of the war during which time the SAS were in some form of heavy contact with the enemy on virtually a daily basis. This was no accident. The enemy was clearly seeking out the Australian force in a coordinated and well drilled fashion, whilst at the same time the SAS were intentionally meeting him head-on with unpredictable shock engagements. However, the enemy couldn't keep pace with this high-tempo shock activity and were ultimately beaten in this phase.

Australian SAS troopers patrolling in heavily armed All Terrain Vehicles. Vehicles like these were very effective in repelling fierce Iraqi offensives.

On the second night in Iraq, a good proportion of the SAS force was involved in a raid on what turned out to be a well-defended radio relay station. This was a carefully coordinated activity that involved a very methodical ground and airborne surveillance process that collected as much information about the site as possible prior to the attack phase of the operation. The attack used carefully placed cut-offs and a sequenced assault to clear the facility, followed by close air support to destroy the tower. Surprise was achieved and a sharp, but one-sided, firefight ensued with a significant number of enemy casualties; the net result being the destruction of the facility. This operation immediately decreased the Iraqi theatre ballistic missile capability and also sent a very strong message to the Iraqi leadership in Baghdad.

Australians move carefully and tactically through enemy territory.

An example of a night time firefight as seen through Night Vision. Here an Australian opens fire on a target using Night Goggles.

As expected, this activity stirred up a hornets' nest, and on the following morning an SAS element was involved in a running firefight for a significant number of hours. They were engaged by five or six armed vehicles, but the SAS used superior tactical manoeuvres and an application of heavy weapons to destroy most of the force. The enemy, in disarray, eventually withdrew through a number of buildings, but they were pursued by well-directed close air support and were ultimately defeated.

Throughout this firefight and other firefights, the enemy were engaged by the SAS using a significant number of weapons. They included Javelin rocket launchers, heavy machine guns, Mark 19 grenade launchers and sniper rifles. This heavy use of firepower, coupled with the aggressive front foot approach of the SAS, and extensive use of close air support, was enough to break the spirit of the most demanding enemy assault.

On a separate occasion in the first few days, another small element was confronted with a force of about fifty enemy mounted in civilian four-wheel drive vehicles and trucks. This force aggressively assaulted the Australians using rocket-propelled grenades, mortars and machine guns but to no avail, as the SAS held their ground; a remarkable feat considering that their weapons systems had suffered numerous stoppages at the height of the firefight. Within minutes of the contact, the Iraqi vehicles were destroyed, forcing their occupants to dismount and fight on foot, which made them extremely vulnerable. The SAS, seeing their plight, pushed forward aggressively and routed them. It was here that one soldier, due to a weapon stoppage, used all four of the available weapon systems mounted on his long-range patrol vehicle.

'Systematically moving from weapon system to weapon system, he was able to engage the enemy targets at vastly different ranges in different circumstances. Certainly testament to the skill of the SAS soldier', said Colonel John Mansell.

There were a number of other engagements similar to this in the first three or four days, which quite clearly set the enemy on the back foot from the outset

Cause and effect. Coalition fighters hurry to engage the enemy. Below: a photograph showing a direct hit on an enemy target. The SAS were able to call in air strikes at any time to take out enemy vehicles and positions.

and from which they didn't recover. The intensity of this phase was such that the SAS were on full throttle without any real sleep for ninety-six hours. In contrast to this frantic pace, another SAS element had been concealed in observation positions overlooking Highway Ten, and testament to their skill, they remained undetected throughout the period. This was a significant and equally demanding task given the environmental demands, the numbers of enemy around and also the nomadic Bedouin that move around in this area. The contrast was striking.

'On the one hand, there were elements of the SAS moving at a million miles an hour, daily engaging the enemy with aggressive firefights. And, on the other hand, we have a separate force operating with equal skill, equal daring, but with great skill and great stealth,' said Colonel Mansell.

In the early stages of the campaign it was apparent that the kilometre 160 feature, which is essentially a cross roads and a truck stop, needed to be neutralized and at one stage upwards of 200 Iraqis defended the feature. The SAS, using high-powered optics and standing off from the target, called in air support to pinpoint targets over a forty-eight hour period to destroy the facility.

They then assembled a large vehicle-mounted force to assault and clear the installation.

'*Unfortunately, but as expected, the remaining enemy had withdrawn under cover of a sandstorm,*' said Colonel Mansell.

The SAS standoff capability, as agents for air power, was critical to provide pinpoint guidance against targets which were indistinguishable from the air. Just as importantly, the SAS were also able to confirm that targets had indeed been neutralized. The enemy's pro-active and coordinated counter special operations tactics that could have worked so well against an ill-prepared force, were largely ineffective in the face of such an exceptionally aggressive and well equipped force who fought a high tempo war at a high tempo pace,' said an Australian Army officer.

At this point it was clear that the enemy's ability to launch theatre ballistic missiles from the west had been neutralized. The psychological impact was also significant upon the Iraqis. Quite clearly they were unhinged. It was the Special Forces tactic to achieve this and this they did in a highly effective manner.

About a week into the campaign the area quietened down and the SAS became more and more involved in highway interdiction tasks. Basically the task here was to deny the enemy any form of escape route, be it for high value mobile targets or regime personnel, while at the same time being mindful of the suicide bomber threat. In order to achieve operational effectiveness, they had to constantly change their locations and methods so as not to set a pattern and give the opposition the opportunity to prepare themselves with some sort of suicide bomb capability. They experienced success on a number of occasions culminating in the capture of a significant number of likely Fedayeen and Ba'ath

Party members, along with considerable amounts of cash as they tried to exit the country. They also apprehended convoys carrying communications equipment and gasmasks. Also during this period they established links with the local sheiks from the enemy occupied town of Ar Ramadi which helped facilitate the capitulation of the enemy in this location.

The last significant activity involving the SAS was the capture of the massive Al Asad air base, one of Iraq's largest. The SAS found it defended and occupied by a large force, in the order of 100 or so armed looters, requiring comprehensive and forceful operations to secure it.

'*The operation therefore, required both boldness*

Under new Australian management. The tail fin of a Russian made Iraqi MIG fighter. None of the Iraqi Airforces' fighters ever left the ground during the conflict and none were bombed.

Members of 4 RAR cautiously approach a well camouflaged Iraqi fighter at Al Asad airbase.

and cunning for such a small number in the Special Forces Task Group to take such a large air base manned by such a large number of forces. In one engagement, to avoid unnecessary casualties and despite being engaged by the looters' heavy weapons, the SAS Commander had ordered his snipers to place well-aimed shots quite close to the looters to scare them away. Fortunately, it had the desired effect,' said Colonel Mansell.

Upon securing the base, they conducted a very lengthy and potentially highly dangerous room by room clearance of the facility. There was always the danger of mines and booby traps and, when taken into consideration with the size of the base, it is little surprise that it took some thirty-six hours to clear.

'The facility contained in excess of fifty MIG jets, and 7.9 million kilograms of explosive ordnance. While the SAS were operating to secure the air base, Royal Australian Air Force F/A-18 fighter jets provided over watch. Shortly afterwards, the Commandos and the

An Australian F/A-18 fighter jet, returns from a close air support patrol.

Incident Response Regiment came in to assist securing and searching the base. Over the following days the Task Group cleared and repaired the runways to allow an air link to be established and the first fixed wing aircraft into Al Asad was an Australian 36 Squadron C-130 aircraft,' said Colonel Mansell.

Significantly, at this point probably the largest gathering of Australian Special Operations Forces ever deployed into hostile territory was gathered at Al Asad with appropriate support being provided by Royal Australian Air Force fighter and transport aircraft. This was a very proud moment for the Special Forces Task Group and the Australian Defence Force, as they had both performed superbly.

ACCOUNT BY ROYAL MARINE AT AL FAW

'My personal war with Iraq, started in the early hours of the first night of the invasion phase-but nearly ended that night also on account of a minefield. It was a really weird experience for me and all the lads- first it was hurry up and wait, then warp 9 . . . followed by stop. The insertion phase had gone well enough, but when we landed that's when it went, well tits up to put it bluntly. It was pitch black where we were, and apart from some lights in the dim and distant there was nothing to see. Some of the lads had NVGs, which is just as well as they were the ones who spotted the fucking mines that were near us. The boss shouted at us not to move, as he wanted us to wait until first light, which made sense to me as I couldn't see fuck all - and I'm sure he couldn't either - also I don't like mines. I found a spot to lay up in, which was on a beach with a small raised bit- the theory being it would give me some cover if we had a contact- but if we was mortared, then I was going to get FUBARED (Fucked up beyond all recognition). For me it was the longest four hours of my fucking life, I can tell you, but we all got through it. At one stage we did have a laugh when some Muppet shouted for everyone to be quiet as we were tactical. Picture the scene, here we all are sat put on account of these mines- with helicopters whizzing over us all night long to the west- jets whizzing over us to the east and this numpty wants us to be quiet . . . Fuck off!!!!

'If the Iraqis didn't know we were here now, then they never would. As daylight slowly broke

An example of a coalition soldier using his NVGs to which many of the Allied Forces probably owe their lives.

Royal Marine Commandos on board HMS *Ark Royal*, prepare to be deployed into the Al Faw peninsula.

through we could see where we all were, and more importantly where the mines were. I could see three of them in and around our location-but there were way more further down the beach. The boss seemed to reckon that they had been placed earlier in the night before we arrived as they weren't buried - but at least they were visible, that's the most important point. After a long night I just wanted to push on, but we were told there was to be no move until later in the morning as we were to await other units. Eventually after what seemed like an eon, we began to move out of our position and forward towards a distant column of smoke that was rising up on the horizon. By now it was like Piccadilly Circus here, we had helicopters flying over us all the time-some with underslung loads and others just moving troops I guess. High above them there were jet contrails- but what aircraft types they were, I have no idea. As I looked around me I felt proud, as all I could see everywhere was military activity- loads of it, and all ours thankfully. At one stage we saw a large column of US troops moving forward towards an urban area that was west of us and obviously under attack- I say that as we could hear small arms fire and the thud of explosions coming from there. Shortly after we passed this location, we came across a small group of Iraqi children, complete with adults who seemed really pleased to see us. One of them tried to talk to us in broken English, but wasn't really sure of what he was saying. I made a friendly gesture to him and gave him my boiled sweets and chocolate bars- as they were beginning to melt due to the intense mid-day heat -

but to him it was Christmas come early. We continued our move forward, and were joined by other commandos and some US Marines. These lads had already been in a firefight and were keen to find another- so were we as we hadn't seen any combat at this point. In fact our first engagement didn't occur until late in the evening of the first day- but it was worth the wait- as everything that I had ever trained for was to come into play. The attack itself was against a group of crappy looking buildings on the outside of an urban area located near an old port facility. The boss told us that it been attacked earlier in the day, but was still active- as the US Marines had come under effective fire from there on a number of occasions during the afternoon. In support we had no armour-which is fucking typical, and no artillery as everything was committed elsewhere. However, what we did have was an American Marine Cobra gunship that was on hand in case things got a bit hot, which was rather cool if I may say so. As my section moved forward to the side of the road which was out of sight of the target buildings by way of a bank of old rocks, wrecked cars and general junk, the shooting started. It started off heavy at first, then went quiet, then started up again - but seemed to have no cohesion. I had an LSW, and used the SUSAT on it to try and spot the rag head that was firing at us, but saw nowt. What didn't help was the dust blowing in front of our position-as you could see fuck all - but it must have been the same for them (the Iraqis) as well, as their shooting was bollocks. We had a sniper with us who was a bit tasty, and he was put up to try and spot for us. Just as he was getting into position we had a bit of a result, as a number of Iraqis ran out of one building and over towards another- shooting as they went. As they did so, just about every swinging dick in the place opened fire on them- causing 'em to hit the dirt. They were now really in the shit, as they couldn't move forward or back without being slotted- we had 'em. Overhead the Cobra buzzed them, but didn't fire as we were all too close to where the Iraqis were.

A USMC Cobra rides shotgun for British Royal Marines in Umm Qasr.

A British Royal Marine Commando sniper provides cover for his colleagues through the sight of his L96 A1 rifle.

'Eventually, one of the lads shouted that they were surrendering as they had thrown their weapons out onto the open area between the buildings and the nearby road- but there was no white flag. After a while it dawned on us that they may not have one, so one of us shouted out to surrender- but with the noise of the chopper above it all got drowned out. As we waited out, one of them got up with his hands above his head and began walking slowly forward towards us. His move was quickly followed by the others who joined him-and with the help of the Yanks that were with us, we took their surrender. Looking at them, they were shit scared- and probably conscripts as well, as their weapon handling skills were abysmal. Once documented, we moved forward towards the buildings in arrow head-as we thought there might be more of them, but there weren't. What amazed me, was the fact that with all the lead flying in their direction, not one of them got hit-which is something you wouldn't expect.

A British soldier checks out a captured cache of Iraqi weapons and ammunition.

'Inside the buildings we found loads of shit, ranging from RPG rounds to mortar shells-all nasty stuff- but no more Iraqis. My guess is that the ones we captured were not the same as the ones who had attacked the Yanks earlier in the day-as they were a bit good, and these ones weren't. Anyway that's my war story for you.'

COMBAT REPORT FROM SOMEWHERE IN NORTHERN IRAQ SOLDIER D

'As the dawn broke over our position, the morning after our night insertion, I was fascinated by our surrounding area as it reminded me of Afghanistan. Apart from the birds flying over the valley in front of us, and squawking every now and again it was totally quiet - there was just no way that you would believe a war was taking place barely spitting distance from the position we were occupying. The week before we'd been just north of Mosul, where there was intense Iraqi Army activity but for us no contacts. Our general mission was to see and report, nothing else. For us it was just a question of finding targets, reporting them and then observing them to see if anything interesting was happening.

'One night, just a few klicks from our position an almighty 'mother' of a firefight developed on a ridgeline opposite our OP. At first we couldn't tell if the fire was for us or someone else, but after a while it became apparent that the Iraqis were shooting at each other. We later learned that some had deserted their positions and fled towards the Kurdish enclaves, and that the firing was designed to deter others who had the same idea.

'I found this area a bizarre place to operate in as there was something of a phoney war taking place. By that I mean there was no all out fighting, yet there was no peace either, it seemed that the Iraqis were resigned to the fact that they were going to lose this war and they didn't want to fall foul of the Kurds, especially with Saddam gone.'

ACCOUNT BY SAS OPERATIVE

'Unlike the rest of the guys who were hard at it in western Iraq, we were, for our sins, on a covert recce mission in the middle of nowhere- at least that's how it felt at first. Basically our team was a road-watch team, but to call what we were observing a road would be an insult- this was no M1. Our mission tasking was simply to watch, report and target, but with the type of traffic we had to observe targeting would have been a waste of time, as the munitions would cost more than the target itself. For the best part of the day, all that moved down here was smugglers and their ill-gotten gains - they carried oil, tyres, satellite dishes and just about anything else that would bring in a buck-or in this case a dinar. But for us this was good news, as the Iraqis tended to turn a blind eye to this sort of activity-making movement for us easier should we be compromised. Military traffic seemed limited to troop, artillery and armour movements-but no Scuds. Even at night, little changed apart from the volume of traffic, we certainly never saw any target of value that would justify compromising our position here. As boring and unexciting as our traffic was, it told us where Saddam's forces were moving to-so to somebody this was good intelligence. During our time here nothing really threatened our security as we were on a high embankment that only goats, or idiots like us would climb and visit. The only time we had a concern, was when a camel caravan traversed across the side of our embankment about 80 metres away. However the herders had other things on their minds, as they were trying to transport the carcass of a luxury car downhill without losing it off the camels' backs. The saying "the straw that broke the camel's back" seemed to come to mind at the time, but in this case it was a Merc. For the others in my team it was a great laugh, as it helped break the monotony of the situation - but I had seen this stunt performed before- only in Afghanistan and not Iraq. Once the herders had moved on, normality returned to the OP - but things were about to change. The war was well underway by now, and the military movements on the road were intensifying by the hour-first one way and then another-but still no Scuds or anything else that could pass off as a high threat. There were certainly no Weapons of Mass Destruction here. Barely a week later and there was clearly an exodus of Iraqi head sheds, as the pressure was mounting and they knew it. I personally had no beef with the rank and file Iraqi Army - as they were as much victims of Saddam's regime as anyone else- it was the Republican Guard and the Fedayeen who I despised - as they persecuted their own people.

Soldiers of Saddam's evil Republican Guard. They were the most feared and hated members of Saddam's war machine, being both fierce and fanatical in equal proportion.

A British TACBE emergency radio.

'The only time that our lives were ever potentially threatened, was during an over flight by American close support aircraft, that just happened to be in our vicinity as a convoy was passing through. They lined up for an attack, but thankfully broke off. I say thankfully because we probably would have got malleted as well as the Iraqis, as we were very close to the road.

'If things had really gone 'Pete Tong' we could have tried calling them off by way of the TACBE , but then we would have risked being compromised. And I personally did not fancy trogging off into the Ulu, with half of Saddam's cousins on my tail . . . as they just might be a little miffed.'

BRITISH SF OPERATIVE

'From the time the balloon first went up we were busy, real busy. We were initially deployed close to Basra, and had the job of targeting Iraqi forces- both conventional and unconventional. Our position was such that we had a good field of view over the main urban area that led to the river, and as such we could observe everything that moved along the main line of communication. This vantage point gave us the ability to recce or target an area as circumstances dictated, as we had a commanding view over the city. On several occasions this vista provided us with good intelligence on Iraqi troop and armour movements, as we were able to predict their routes out of the city - thus enabling an intercept by friendly forces or a target mission.

'Our team was one of several that had infiltrated the city of Basra- and between us we had all routes covered. In one action we spotted a small convoy of armed Toyota pick-up trucks heading for a warehouse complex that was located near to a bridge controlled by British and US

A British Challenger tank provides cover in Basra. These were a welcome sight for coalition forces, as they were able to deal with Iraqi armoured vehicles and armoured personnel carriers.

forces. As we observed it, a group of Iraqis set up a mortar on the back of one of the vehicles and began bracketing the bridge with effective fire. Seeing the danger, we were able to provide target information on the convoy via our FAC - and within a very short time the threat was eliminated. In another action, we spotted a large force of some twenty Iraqi armoured personnel carriers and tanks heading for our forces surrounding the city. But our concern was short lived, as the force was quickly destroyed by a squadron of Challenger tanks. For the Iraqis this must have been an extremely frustrating time, as they could not move anywhere within the city without SF spotting them. Essentially we acted as a barometer for our own forces - gauging the right time for them to attack, and gauging the right time for them to withdraw, and only when we felt that the time was right did they advance. I believe that our actions saved many lives-both British and Iraqi alike, and I am proud of what we did.'

THE SBS

One of the most bizarre incidents to occur during Operation Iraqi Freedom was that of a compromised mission involving the British SBS, the bizarre part being its similarity to the Bravo Two-Zero story of the first Gulf War.

The incident occurred some weeks after the initial invasion phase of the war, when a small eight-man SBS mobility patrol, operating in northern Iraq near the vicinity of Mosul, was discovered by a large force of Iraqi troops, believed to be Republican Guards. Under normal combat conditions, they would have simply bugged out and made their way to a pre-arranged RV point but this was not possible, as the Iraqi forces had blocked off all available exit points leading from the road that they were on. Those that were not covered by troops were impassable due to steep sided hills and deep ravines.

As they contemplated a course of action, the Iraqi troops opened fire on them from all sides, which immediately prompted an SBS response. Although the SOV (Special Operations Vehicle) Land-Rovers that the SBS were using, were extremely well armed they were, however, no match for such a formidable opposing force.

Fearing the worst, the SBS debussed from their vehicles and made a tactical withdrawal to the nearby hills, as that seemed the better option at the time. With the Iraqis hot on their heels they decided to split up into smaller groups, as this would give them a better chance of survival.

In part their theory was correct, as the main body of the group managed to give their pursuers the slip relatively quickly and, once completely clear, were soon extracted by a rescue force sent in earlier by helicopter. For the other two

A heavily armed British Special Operations Vehicle (SOV) patrols the desert. Note the Milan launcher on top of the vehicle.

members of the group however, things were not going so well, as they had missed the rescue RV point and were now running for their lives towards Syria with, it would appear, half the Iraqi Army in pursuit. At one stage, the Arab TV network Al-Jazeera, broadcast a report showing Iraqis driving around in a British Army Land-Rover, but these reports were dismissed by the British MOD as being mere Iraqi propaganda, the official line being that the vehicle had been jettisoned from a Chinook helicopter following an engine problem. After this story broke, nothing more was heard about the incident for several weeks until the end of the war, when it emerged via the British Government that the two SBS men had made it to Syria, and that they were safe.

It transpired, that following intense government-to-government negotiations they were sent back home to the UK discreetly, and all at a time when tensions were running high between America and Syria. It was a remarkable story and yet again showed what these Special Forces operatives are made of.

UK HELICOPTER SPECIAL OPERATIONS

Although the UK does not have a direct equivalent to the US 160th SOAR, it does have an equal to the 101st Airborne (Air Assault) Division, albeit a smaller one, courtesy of 16 Air Assault Brigade. Unlike our American cousins, the UK simply does not have the helicopter assets of the United States. On the first night of Operation Iraqi Freedom, nobody would have believed that, as all the stops were pulled out to create the illusion of a massive air armada. *'The air assault on the Al Faw peninsula was unique, I've never seen helicopters used so aggressively in a plan'*, said Wing Commander David Prowse, Officer Commanding 18 Squadron, after he had led the first wave of Boeing Chinook HC2s through fierce sandstorms during the opening hours of the invasion phase. Their mission was to land Royal Marine Commandos on strategically valuable oil facilities and was made all the more difficult by the fact that the landing zones were being bombarded by both mortar and artillery fire. In part this counter-action had been anticipated in

37

British Commandos deploy on the AL Faw Peninsula, courtesy of an RAF Chinook helicopter.

advance by the coalition Special Forces, who had taken steps to neutralize their effect. In one such mission, a CH -46E Sea Knight returning from Al-Faw was lost in a non-combat related accident, resulting in the loss of four crew and eight British soldiers (some of whom were believed to be SBS). Prowse further stated,

'We have been used in so many roles, over a large area of southern Iraq, that we felt fully involved. When I first briefed my inner circle on the plan, there was stunned silence; after two months training, everyone was ready for it. The plan changed very little- it flew as briefed to me. We knew the risks - that gave us a high confidence level.'

In part his confidence was understandable, as the coalition forces had little fear of the Iraqi Air Force: their operational capability had been heavily degraded prior to the outbreak of hostilities. In total, the UK deployed some ninety-seven helicopters on Operation Telic, a large force that was split into three distinct force packages.

PACKAGE 1: was deployed with a tailored air group embarked on the HMS *Ark Royal* Task Group.

An RAF Chinook carries out cross-decking duties, a mundane but necessary task.

A British Royal Marine Lynx lifts off the deck of its carrier for a destination unkown. Although not as well armed as American attack helicopters, the Lynx was highly efficient in many roles other than that of a dedicated attack helicopter.

PACKAGE 2: was deployed to Jordan, to support British, Australian and US Special Forces operating in western Iraq.

PACKAGE 3: was deployed to Kuwait to support the main land force, after Ankara turned down a UK request to base its forces in Turkey for operations against northern Iraq.

All helicopters for this force, except for those operating from Royal Navy warships were provided by the Joint Helicopter Command (JHC) which is based at Wilton, Wiltshire. They were delegated to operate with the three British Brigades deployed in the Middle East and were organized as follows.

3 Regiment Army Air Corps (AAC) was to operate under 16 Air Assault Brigade's tactical control, while RAF Chinooks and Puma HC1s were to support

A Royal Marine Gazelle takes off on a Recce mission following reports of enemy activity.

A Royal Marine offloads a Quad bike onboard HMS *Ocean*.

7 Armoured, 3 Commando and 16 Air Assault Brigades.

'*We are a brigade - level force- 1,500 people- making it the biggest thing for RAF support helicopters since the last Gulf War,*' stated JHF HQ commander Group Captain Andy Pulford. He went on to say,

'*The Al Faw operation was the largest helicopter assault since Vietnam. There were 42 helicopters in the air at one point. It was the first time since the Falklands that we had to use all of the complete helicopter force (except for the RAF's Merlin HC3s) at the same time. The whole fleet has been out doing its job.*'

During the war itself, UK helicopters performed just about every possible mission from air assault to stores replenishment. They were extremely active around Al Faw, Basra and the western desert, where they supported Special Forces operations in difficult and demanding conditions. Other roles included POW transportation, anti-armour and Eagle patrols; a well tried and tested method of suppressing insurgents by means of air power.

For the British, this special operation was a remarkable success, as it enabled them to deploy the main combat elements of 3 Commando Brigade on heavily defended enemy coastline in hours, rather than days as would have been the case if they had chosen to rely on landing craft. Later in the war as British forces stormed the Iraqi city of Basra, helicopters were used for attacking buildings, vehicles, armour, artillery, gunboats and troops. But their finest hour took place on the Rumailah oil fields, as British and US forces secured the key oil wells that Saddam had threatened to blow up as part of his scorched earth policy. Despite the Iraqis' best attempts to destroy the

British troops burst out of an RAF Chinook during a deployment exercise.

An RAF Chinook crew decide to take an extra GPMG for protection on a mission. At times, these helicopters carried more weaponry than the supposed attack helicopters assigned to protect them.

wells they failed, as the British and Americans were simply too quick for them. In part this agility was down to the services of the RAF's Pumas and the AAC's Lynx helicopters, as they enabled the British forces to deploy rapidly from location to location when tasked with providing mobile vehicle checkpoints and security patrols. Flying helicopters at low level and at night is demanding enough at the best of times, but in sand and dust storms it is something else. To the eternal credit of the pilots, they overcame all of these problems admirably, performing with great skill and tenacity in conditions that were, at times, utterly appalling.

Despite being targeted by Iraqi gunners on numerous occasions, no British helicopters were lost to enemy fire but two were badly damaged, one Chinook after it ran out of fuel while en route to Baghdad and another Chinook after being shot at while flying reinforcements into Al Majar Al Kabir, following the ambush of a Parachute Regiment patrol on 24 June 2003. Overall, the Chinook performed superbly during the second Gulf War, prompting one senior officer to comment,

'In the first wave on to Al Faw, we delivered 220 Marines in four aircraft- it would have taken 22 Sea Kings to deliver them. When the assault was delayed, the Sea Kings with us had to go into a holding pattern and then go back to a forward arming and refuelling point or ships to refuel.'

One other officer, Wing Commander Paul Lyall, OC 33 Squadron stated,

'This operation proved you need varying sizes of helicopters. In vehicle checkpoint operations, we carried eight to twelve troops. That is

41

insignificant for the Chinook but right for a Puma. Its simplicity and ruggedness made the Puma ideal for this environment. It is a risk judgement. Do you have fifty troops in one target or spread them around four or five targets? You need more smaller helicopters along-side the big helicopters. The Puma is good for covert tasks, the Chinook is a larger beast; noisy and a target.'

TASK FORCE 20 - KILLING THE HYDRA

Following the fall of Baghdad in April 2003 and the supposed ending of hostilities, coalition forces embarked on a series of operations to find Saddam Hussein and his sons Uday, Qusay and Ali, as their demise was seen as being critical to the long term stability of Iraq.

For all concerned these were tough operations, as US forces were being subjected to numerous attacks each day, by radical elements such as the Fedayeen Saddam and the terrorist group 'The Return'. As each day went by during the months of May and June 2003, US losses increased throughout central and northern Iraq, so much so that there were now serious concerns as to how long America could continue with its casualty rate, which was now running at virtually one fatality per day. Desperate to get a result, America set

Like father like son. Saddam's sons, Uday and Qusay, were a chip off the old block.

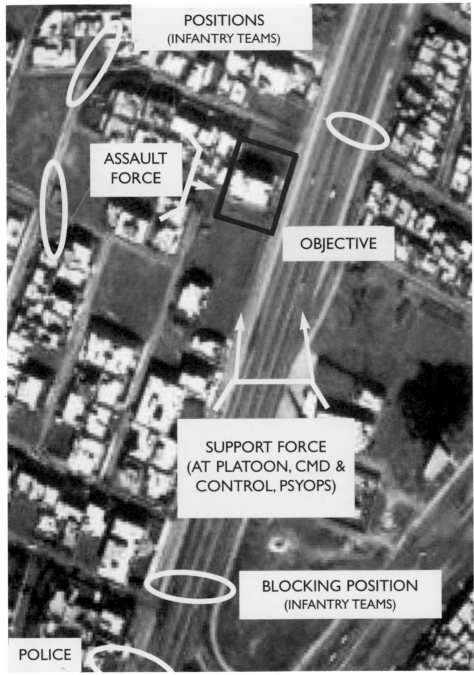

POSITIONS
(INFANTRY TEAMS)

ASSAULT FORCE

OBJECTIVE

SUPPORT FORCE
(AT PLATOON, CMD & CONTROL, PSYOPS)

BLOCKING POSITION
(INFANTRY TEAMS)

POLICE

The scene of the last stand from the air, showing the deployment of US Forces prior to the assault phase of the operation.

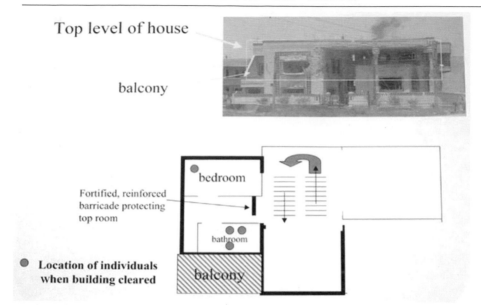

Top level of house

balcony

Fortified, reinforced
barricade protecting
top room

bedroom

bathroom

● Location of individuals
when building cleared

balcony

Photo and layout of the building from where Uday and Qusay made their last stand.

up a reward programme in Iraq that was similar in scope to that operated in Afghanistan, the idea being cash for information: $25,000,000 for the whereabouts of Saddam Hussein and $15,000,000 for his sons, Uday and Qusay. Shortly after the reward was posted US forces in the region began receiving numerous bogus and unreliable reports of possible Saddam sightings, or 'Elvis sightings' as they became known, but all turned out to be false. Indeed, there were many innocent Iraqis who longed for Saddam to be caught as they were being arrested on account of their facial likeness to him. Ironically, the most arrested man in Iraq was Saddam's distant cousin, an impoverished petrol pump attendant from Tikrit, who hated Saddam with a passion, as he had jailed him in the past for refusing to be one of his many doubles.

However in July 2003, a piece of information arrived in the hands of the US Army's Gray Fox unit, that appeared to be both interesting and credible, the informant being none other than a relative of Saddam, Nawaf al-Zaidani, a sheikh of the Bu Issa tribe.

In his statement to Gray Fox, Nawaf al-Zaidani stated that he had unwanted guests in his villa that needed removing - they were Saddam's sons, Uday, the 'ace of hearts' and second on the US list of the fifty-five most wanted Iraqi officials featured on the infamous deck of cards, who was an evil psychopath and reviled member of the Ba'ath party and his brother, Qusay, the 'ace of clubs', and Saddam's successor.

For the Americans, this was an early Christmas present that was just too good to be true and they wasted no time in deploying forces to the region where the villa was located. The forces chosen for this dangerous mission were drawn from the elite Task Force 20.

The villa itself was located in the northern city of Mosul, some 280 miles north of Baghdad, and just outside the 'Sunni-triangle', an area where Saddam still enjoyed strong support, as it served both him and his former regime members as something of a transit point. It was located close to the Syrian border; the reason his sons were also seeking sanctuary there.

On 22 July 2003, some 200 members of the 101st Airborne Division, together with elite SEAL and Delta operatives surrounded the suspect villa, after elements of Gray Fox had confirmed it to be the correct target. Anticipating some form of resistance, both from the occupants of the villa and from the locals, Task Force 20 set up a defensive perimeter. Their assessment of the situation was proven correct after a small team of US soldiers tried to gain access to the building via the front door but were met with a fusillade of automatic gunfire that wounded four of them, forcing a hasty withdrawal. As Task Force 20 took stock of the situation, A-10 Thunderbolt close support aircraft and Apache helicopter gunships began buzzing the villa but were ordered not to fire, as the possibility of a blue-on-blue contact was just too great. Instead, they elected to pulverize the villa with intense firepower, as this option would both minimize casualties and collateral damage. This was a prudent decision, as the villa had been heavily fortified prior to Task Force 20's arrival and with nothing to lose by toughing it out, the occupants were putting up fierce resistance; so much so, that at one stage of the operation, serious consideration was given to calling in

The A10 Thunderbolt and the AH64 Apache attack helicopter (left) were called in as close support for Task Force 20.

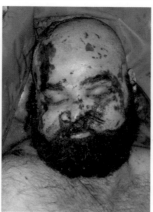

Qusay and Uday Hussein in life and death. An autopsy carried out on the bodies, confirmed that they were the Hussein brothers.

an air strike. The idea was rejected, forcing Task Force 20 to resort to the use of anti-tank missiles instead. Once employed against the villa, the occupants' guns soon fell silent, at which time an all out assault was mounted on the now burning building, by members of the Special Forces. In all, from start to finish, the siege of the villa had lasted for six hours but its after effects would last for weeks, as America had now hurt Saddam personally.

Once the charred bodies had been dragged from the wreckage of the stone-columned villa, an autopsy confirmed that two of the bodies were indeed those of Saddam's sons, Uday and Qusay, while the others were later identified as those of a bodyguard and a young boy, believed to be Qusay's fourteen-year-old son, Mustafa. Other casualties included one Iraqi bystander killed and five others wounded.

According to Lieutenant General Ricardo Sanchez, the head of coalition forces in Iraq, '*We are certain that Uday and Qusay were killed today. We've used multiple sources to identify the individuals.*' He later added that the US expected to pay out the $15 million reward that the Bush administration had offered for information leading to the death or capture of each of Saddam's sons.

US forces eventually buried Uday and Qusay in northern Iraq in the hope that Saddam would come out of hiding to pay his final respects to his sons.

CHAPTER TWO

OPERATION RED DAWN

THE CAPTURE OF SADDAM HUSSEIN

On Sunday, 14 December 2003, America's most senior administrator, Paul Bremer called a press conference and commenced his speech with the words, 'We got him!'

He was, of course, referring to the capture of the world's most wanted man, Saddam Hussein or HVT (High Value Target) No. 1 as he was known within US military and intelligence circles. The capture of Saddam was the result of an intelligence tip-off gleaned from intensive military operations in and around the former dictator's home town of Tikrit in northern Iraq. With a bounty of $25,000,000 on his head, Saddam made for an attractive target, as the payment would be made whether he was found dead or alive. In part his capture was due to intelligence gained from distant relatives and members of the Kurdish PUK, but the role of Special Forces in this operation should not be underestimated as they were the ones who captured him, ironically without a single shot being fired. This was in contrast to the operation that killed his two sons, Uday and Qusay, where a battle raged for almost a day before they were eventually overcome but Saddam went out without so much as a whimper.

CIA images of how Saddam might look post Operation Iraqi Freedom. Ironically these pictures were released shortly before his capture.

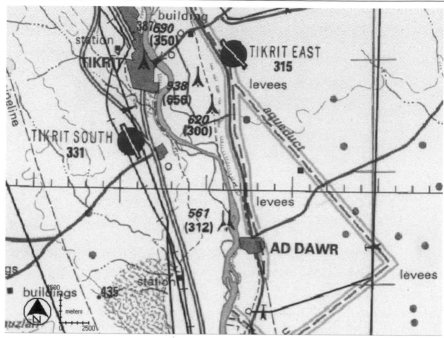

Map of Wolverine 1 and 2 target area.

The remarkable operation that led to his capture unfolded as follows:

10.50 a.m. (7.50 GMT) Saturday: coalition forces received intelligence on the possible location of Saddam Hussein, the target area being the small village of Ad-Dawr, some eleven miles from Tikrit. Two suspect sites were identified as possible hiding places; they were designated under the codename of Wolverine 1 and Wolverine 2.

The operation was to be known as 'Red Dawn' and only the senior commanders knew the intended target, HVT No. 1; for all others concerned it

The objective area. Wolverine 1 and 2 from the air.

Close up of Wolverine I.

was a routine HVT operation.

6 p.m: Under cover of darkness and at high speed, some 600 US soldiers, including elements of Task Force 20 deployed to the target location by means of helicopter and vehicle. The main force was commanded by Colonel Jim Hickey, and comprised the 4th Infantry Division, supported by Humvees, light armour, artillery and Apache helicopter gunships, while the smaller Special Forces element of the force operated under the command and control of Lieutenant General Ricardo Sanchez, the most senior US military commander in Iraq. The

A line drawing showing the cross section of Saddam's spider hole and its location.

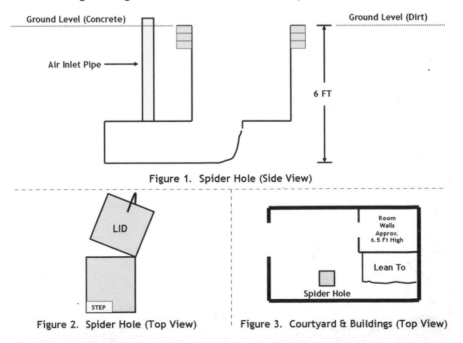

Figure 1. Spider Hole (Side View)

Figure 2. Spider Hole (Top View)

Figure 3. Courtyard & Buildings (Top View)

force commander was given the mission; 'Kill or capture HVT No. 1.'

8 p.m: US forces surround and secure the village of Ad-Dawr and commence 'sweep and clear' operations. After an initial sweep, which revealed nothing, the soldiers cordoned off an area of land, one mile square, and commenced a thorough and detailed search. After a short period, a suspicious location was found to the north-west of Wolverine2, its appearance being that of a small walled compound with a metal lean-to and a mud hut. As operators from Task Force 20 made their approach to the target, two Iraqis fled the location. They were later identified as Saddam's bodyguards. Now the operators began a finger tip search of the area, until a rug was found covering a fake rock bed of bricks and earth that was built into a block of polystyrene, its purpose being to act as a hatch cover.

8.26 p.m: As the Special Forces cautiously removed the hatch, a spider hole was discovered that led to a shaft some eight feet deep. Now pointing their weapons into the shaft and illuminating it by means of torches, they discovered a figure lurking within. It was Saddam Hussein.

Looking dirty, haggard and dishevelled, the once feared and arrogant dictator was now reduced to a pathetic figure. He appeared 'tired and resigned' said Sanchez, while Major General Ray Odiero stated,

My, How the mighty fall!

'He was caught like a rat; he was disorientated as he came up, then he was just very much bewildered, then he

The many faces of Saddam Hussein.

Saddam the tyrant.   **Saddam the tramp.**   **Saddam the timid.**

Mission accomplished! After the success of Operation Red Dawn, President George W. Bush breaks the news of Saddam Hussein's capture to the American people.

The Ace of Spades. The capture of Saddam was to become a major boost for all coalition forces, although more trouble was to come.

was taken away. He didn't say hardly anything at all. There was no resistance of any sort. They got him out of there very quickly once we figured out who it was. The soldiers were extremely happy and extremely excited, but very professional. It is rather ironic that he was in a hole in the ground across the river from one of these great palaces he built, where he robbed all the money from the Iraqi people.'

9.15 p.m: Saddam is extracted by helicopter and flown to a secure location for medical examination, DNA testing and interrogation.

The lair Saddam left behind was a purpose built bolt-hole, eight feet in length and just large enough to allow a man to lay down flat. It had a small pipe and a fan for ventilation but no communications equipment. Therefore Saddam could not have orchestrated attacks on coalition forces from here. Above the bolt-hole within the hut, two AK-47 assault rifles and a green metal

51

case with $750,000 in $100 dollar bills was discovered, while within the hole itself a pistol was found. Nearby were two small boats, possibly used for transportation and re-supply via the Tigris River, while an old battered taxi parked in the grounds, served as Saddam's limousine. It was a major come down for a man who once lived in opulence and splendour beyond most people's wildest dreams. No doubt, in due course, the people of Iraq will wish to see this tyrant tried and punished for the decades of suffering that he inflicted upon them.

Although the capture of Saddam is a major boost for coalition forces, it is unlikely to bring about total peace and reconciliation but it does bring it a step closer.

CHAPTER THREE

THE
OPERATORS

ACCOUNT BY US SPECIAL FORCES OPERATIVE IN BAGHDAD

'**S**ince this piss-ant war ended, I've been out looking for Mr Saddam Hussein - but I guess that he's gone kinda quiet lately - a bit like Mr Bin Laden. I have to say that I don't care for this place too much, as nobody seems to give a shit for us. Don't get me wrong, I don't expect them to kiss our feet or anything else like that - all I ask is for a bit of respect to be shown to us for what we did over here - it ain't too much to ask. It's not like we're the British who once had an Empire out here - we're Americans and we bring freedom - there's no other agenda. I say these things because I want to know why these guys are attacking us every goddam day.

'*Did we piss them off about something else that I don't know about - or is it just their way of saying - We don't like you in our country, get the message? They're not all bad I guess, but how do you tell the difference?*

'*Take the other day, we were on a sweep and clear mission to the west of the city- driving along a highway that was just ambush boulevard to me - and some local militia opened fire on us. I spotted them straight away, but couldn't fire on them from my vehicle as there were young children playing nearby. The front Humvee however did fire on them - but they got away through a maze of buildings that were in front of us - and for us to pursue them would have been a waste of time as they all basically look the same in a crowd.*

'*Our mission itself however, was not wasted as we found weapons that had been hidden for a future strike against us - but now they were under new ownership -so to speak. Just occasionally we do get lucky out here and drop some bad guys but for the most part the fighting is started by them and not us. One thing I've got to say that really bugs*

The difficulties of urban warfare. American troops cautiously patrol streets heavily populated with children.

me out here is the way in which things are reported. Yes, we do have bad days out here but we also do have a lot of good. Take the infamous deck of cards as an example. Look how many of those 'sons of bitches' we caught already but nobody ever gives us credit for that, no Sir. Compared to our coalition partners, we got the shit end of the stick, and not them. The British have it a little easier in the south, as those folk were never fans of Saddam's in the first place - but up here it's real different as it's his seat of power. He may be gone in presence, but these folk really fear him - you can really pick up on it when you speak to them - they're real scared still. I don't blame them as they still feel that he is here in the city - maybe they're right - as we still haven't caught him yet - as this city is a real maze. I remember one guy showing me what looked like a store - but when my team entered it - what do you know, it's a bunker - complete with tun-

A uniformed Iraqi soldier walks away from a knocked out American tank as men in civilian clothes celebrate, holding AK47s.

nels. *When we searched it, it took ages as it was just so big - kinda recalled me of Afghanistan: man, they had tunnels there too. The tunnels beneath Baghdad are truly massive - not so much in height and width but in length - they go on for miles. When we first searched them we had help from other units within TF 20 - some even from the British SF guys - but we found no trace of Mr Saddam Hussein - I guess he left town when he heard we were coming.'*

101ST AIRBORNE DIVISION (AIR ASSAULT)

The 101st Airborne Division is the biggest air cavalry unit in the world today, and played a key role in Operation Iraqi Freedom. This is their story.

From the time the 101st Airborne Division (Air Assault) first left its forward operating base in the Kuwaiti desert, right up until its arrival in the northern Iraqi city of Mosul, a distance of some 1,200 kilometres, it was in the thick of the action, firing an amazing 3,500 rounds of artillery along the way.

During a briefing given by the division's commander, Major General David H. Petraeus, in which he described their drive north, he stated:

'Our soldiers had a number of very tough fights in southern Iraq, liberating Al Najaf, Karbala and Al Hillah, and then clearing Al Mamadia, Escondaria and south Baghdad, as well as Hadithah in the western desert. We then air assaulted 500km. further north to secure and clear Mosul, Tall Afar, Qaiyara and other cities in Nineveh Province. Three of the division's soldiers were killed in combat and

Heavily armed soldiers of the 101st, take time out during a lull in the fighting.

Kiowa observation helicopter in full flight. These were used in support of ground troops during offensive operations.

some seventy-nine were wounded.

'Mosul had been the scene of some stiff firefights. We came in with a tank battalion, an Apache battalion, a Kiowa squadron and several battalions of infantry, a brigade, and a lot of other combat multipliers, artillery and so forth. We immediately secured the city, establishing a civil military operation centre in the former governance building in the centre of the city, with its leaders, and so forth, to ensure that there weren't repeated instances. We did have several firefights our first week here but we took no casualties.'

As an example of the sheer intensity of the combat in which his units were involved, he stated that they had fired some 3,500 rounds of artillery, nearly 1,000 2.75-inch rockets and Hellfire missiles, 114 tactical missiles and over 40,000 rounds of machine-gun ammunition from Apache and Kiowa attack helicopters. They also used some 150 sorties of close air support, and 'tons of everything else in our inventory'.

'Our Apaches did a great job for us,' said General Petraeus. 'We did in fact change our tactics from night-long deep attack operations, for two reasons. After a successful deep attack, but one in which we crashed a helicopter in a night dust landing on return, and also had problems on take-off we had two problems.

'One was that night dust landings were very, very difficult, and it's despite soldiers who had flown in Afghanistan, spent quite a bit of time with environmental training in Kuwait, had no problems there, and so forth.

'The other problem frankly, was that the Iraqis dispersed very early on and moved their tanks and fighting vehicles and artillery away from the avenues of approach that the 3rd division, in particular, was going to use. And so they weren't massed in the way that we want usually for Apache operations. We did, as I say, have one quite successful deep attack operation, had reasonable battle damage assessment (BDA). But it was not the kind that we had hoped to see with the 100-plus tanks, tracks, artillery and air defense systems.

'Following that, when we could not get the target definition that we needed , we went to daylight, deep armed reconnaissance operations and conducted a number of very successful operations of that type. We packaged these operations with ATACMS missiles, and we called for 114 of these. Each of these clears an entire grid square. They're

massive munitions. We had those in a direct line between the shooters and the Apaches. We also had JSTARS supporting them, to direct them; AWACS, EA-6 jammers, and close air support all packaged together with HARM shooters. And that package went down range; we could identify the target at up to eight kilometres.

'And then, depending on how much fuel the Apache had, if he had a lot of fuel, would bring in close air support, ATACMS, and save his missiles and rockets for later. And then, as he got toward the end of his time on station, find a target, use his munitions, be relieved in place by another platoon or company of Apaches, and do the same thing again and again and again.'

The General said they also had considerable success with attack helicopters operating in close support of infantry soldiers.

'The one operation in which we actually ran into a substantial fight with the Republican Guards, and one of the few cases that I'm aware of where the Republican Guards employed combined arm operations was the morning that the V Corps attacked with an armed recon by our Apaches to the north-west of Karbala, the lake. The 3rd Infantry Division attacked into the Karbala Gap, both in the west and the east of the city and then, of course, really never stopped from there. We attacked into south Al Hillah, where we encountered a dug-in

US soldiers look out for Iraqi troops following an air attack on a nearby position.

US Airborne soldiers patrol cautiously through the streets. Note the tight spacing employed by them compared with the wider spaced patrols used by the British.

Republican Guard battalion with a tank company, with artillery and with air defense, and it fought very, very effectively. We had a very heavy fight there, lost our first soldier.

'The Apache company in that operation fought very, very hard, and took some degree of fire. All of them made it safely back, another sign that the Apache can get hit and just keep on flying, as it showed in Afghanistan as well, in close combat.

'In that fight, we destroyed that Republican Guards' battalion; we destroyed the tank company. We destroyed two artillery battalions, destroyed an artillery battery and a number of other systems. We never again saw a Republican Guard unit stand and fight and employ combined arms like that.'

A member of the 101st kicks his way into a room in search of Iraqi soldiers.

A US Military vehicle brews up following a direct hit.

Evidence of heavy fighting. A building stands wrecked after an air attack.

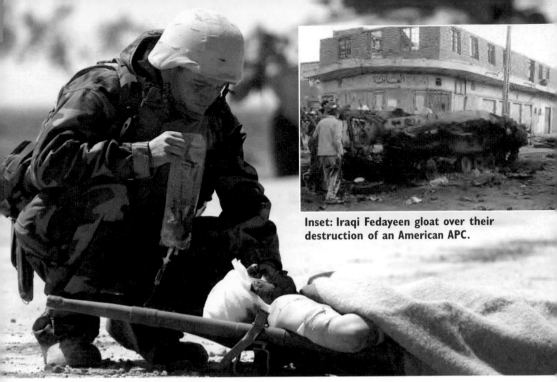

Inset: Iraqi Fedayeen gloat over their destruction of an American APC.

An injured Iraqi soldier receives medical attention after heavy fighting.

General Petraeus also went on to mention that the division often employed its Kiowa Warrior cavalry squadron attack helicopters directly over cities.

'The Kiowas were hard targets to hit generally and could take the doors off and look directly down through the palm trees and into the city streets where the regular army and militia and Fedayeen were hiding their systems, and then using the Apaches around the edge of the city and occasionally bringing them in for really robust attacks. That worked quite successfully.'

THE RESCUE OF PRIVATE FIRST CLASS JESSICA LYNCH

She joined the army to earn money for college and dreamed of eventually becoming a kindergarten teacher. But nowhere in her plans did she ever figure on being captured and held as a POW, only to be rescued in a spectacular manner by her fellow countrymen on 31 March 2003 during Operation Iraqi Freedom.

Like many Americans, Jessica Lynch joined the army as a stepping stone to something else and, as her truck driver father, Gregory Lynch recalled, *'They offered a good deal.'*

The pretty nineteen-year-old from Palestine, West Virginia, joined the army as a supply clerk, and was assigned to the 507th Maintenance Company at Fort Bliss, Texas, a unit comprising welders, repairmen and clerks.

PFC Jessica Lynch prior to her capture.

59

In the early hours of 23 March, the 507th convoy crossed the Iraq-Kuwait border and headed north on the road to Baghdad, their mission being to support the frontline troops. Jessica's amazing story began just three days earlier, when US Marines stormed across the Iraq-Kuwait border, with the 507th following on their tail. However in the confusion of battle, the convoy took a wrong turn and rolled into the southern Iraqi city of Nasiriyah, where they were ambushed by a larger force of Iraqi irregular forces.

The 507th were both outnumbered and outgunned and stood little chance against the enemy forces' overwhelming firepower. After fifteen minutes of intense combat, the guns fell silent leaving nine US soldiers dead and six captured, one of whom was Jessica Lynch.

The face of the enemy. Heavily armed Iraqi fighters pose for the camera.

By the end of the day, the soldiers were officially posted as missing. A few days later, five of the US soldiers that were feared either killed or captured appeared on Iraqi television but there was no sign of Jessica Lynch.

For a while, nothing more was heard, until one day an Iraqi lawyer, identified only as Mohammed, approached a US Marine checkpoint and told them that he had seen an American woman in the Saddam hospital at Nasiriyah. Mohammed, whose wife was a nurse, said: *'I went to the hospital to visit my wife. I could see much more security than normal.'* He then asked one of the

Captured US POWs are paraded on Iraqi TV. The only good to come out of showing such shocking pictures is the fact that they confirm that they are still alive.

doctors who was a friend of his about the extra security, and *'he told me there was a woman American soldier there'*.

Together, the two went to see her. Peering through the hospital room window, Mohammed watched as an Iraqi colonel slapped the injured woman, first with his palm and then with the back of his hand. The lawyer said: *'I knew then I must help her be saved. I decided to tell the Americans.'*

Later that day, after walking for several miles, he came across a US checkpoint. Worried that he'd be mistaken for an attacker in civilian clothes, he approached the Marines with his hands high above his head. When challenged, Mohammed told the Marines: *'I want to help you. I want to tell you important news about Jessica.'* What he told them was immediately passed on to senior officers.

After talking with the Marines, Mohammed returned to the hospital to obtain more information about the security arrangements, such as where they sat to guard the injured American, where they ate and where they slept.

Mohammed said that as he watched what was happening at the hospital, the notorious regime death squad paid an unexpected visit to his home. His wife and six-year-old daughter fled to a nearby family. The squad took his car and other belongings.

Back at the hospital, Mohammed and his friend went into the room where the injured American lay. She was covered up to her chin in a blanket and her head was bandaged. A wound on her right leg was in bad condition. Mohammed said that the doctors wanted to amputate the leg, but he and his doctor friend argued with them and managed to delay the surgery. For two days, Mohammed observed what was going on at the hospital and was able to wish the American *'Good morning'* in English.

When he reported back to the Marines on 30 March, he took five different maps that he and his wife had made. He was able to point to the exact room where the captured soldier was being held. He also gave details of the security layout and the times that shift changes occurred. He had counted forty-one Iraqis involved in guarding the American woman.

Meanwhile, US forces had spent two days planning an operation that was based around the information that Mohammed had provided.

The rescue operation began on the night of 31 March and involved US Army Rangers, Delta Force, US Navy SEALs, USAF pilots and controllers and, for perimeter security, a force of US Marines.

The hospital was on the other side of the river in relation to the disposition of the US forces so a diversion was needed. On a given signal, elements of the US Marines opened fire on known Iraqi positions on the opposite side of the river, while other units sped across the river by means of both helicopters and ground vehicles. As the main assault force moved in to secure the hospital grounds, Special Forces landed nearby and began entering the hospital building where Jessica was being held. As they moved through the building, the SF rescue

The professionals at work. Elite forces employing specialist skills which were tested to the full in the rescue of Jessica Lynch. It was to become a major boost for the morale of all US servicemen serving in Iraq, knowing that highly trained professionals where on standby to embark on daring rescue missions, should the need arise.

team came across a sympathetic doctor who led them straight to Jessica's room. In conversation, he mentioned that there were remains of US troops nearby, either in the morgue or buried outside.

As the Special Forces entered Jessica's room, they called out her name. *'She had been scared, had the sheet up and over her head because she didn't know what was happening,'* said Air Force Major General Victor Renault, when describing the operation five days later.

> *'She lowered the sheet from her head, but didn't really respond. One team member repeated: "Jessica Lynch, we're United States soldiers and we're here to take you home." Jessica seemed to understand that. And as he walked over and took his helmet off, she looked up at him and said, "I'm an American soldier, too".'*

A Ranger doctor evaluated Jessica's condition and the team evacuated her. She seemed in a fair amount of pain. The General said:

> *'Jessica held up her hand and grabbed the Ranger doctor's hand, held on to it for almost the entire time and said "Please don't let anybody leave me." It was clear she knew where she was and didn't want to be left in the hands of the enemy.'*

One helicopter transported her to another nearby waiting aircraft which took her to a field hospital.

Other parts of the rescue team were led to a site where eleven bodies were buried, some of them thought to be American.

> *'The rescue team did not have shovels so they dug up those graves using their hands,'* said the general. *'They wanted to do that very quickly so that they could be off the site before the sun came up.'*

The team recovered the bodies of eight American soldiers and three other people. The American soldiers had been with Jessica when the convoy was attacked.

On Thursday, 3 April Jessica was flown to the US Ramstein Air Base in Germany and was taken to the nearby US Landstuhl Medical Centre. Her

In safe hands. Jessica Lynch manages to smile for the camera after being rescued by US Special Forces.

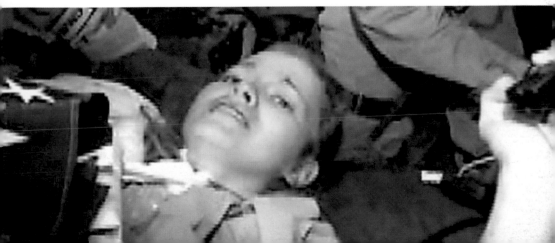

injuries included fractures to her right arm, both legs, right foot and ankle and lumbar spine as well as a head laceration. Doctors initially said that she had not been shot or stabbed, but a few days later, the medical team said that Jessica had been wounded by a low-velocity small calibre weapon.

On Sunday, 6 April Jessica's family arrived at the hospital to see her, having flown from their home in Palestine, West Virginia. On 11 April, Jessica and forty-nine other wounded soldiers arrived at the Andrews Air Force Base outside Washington DC and were taken to a nearby military hospital.

Commenting on the rescue operation afterwards, US Air Force Major General Gene Renuart said,

> 'It's a great testament to the will and desire of our forces to bring their own home.'

ACCOUNT BY US SEAL OPERATIVE

'From the time the war first started, I was on the move virtually 24-7. With our own guys at first, but then later with the British Royal Marines, as they needed us to ride shotgun for them. This tenure of deployment stemmed from a policy of mutual support, where they provided artillery support to our marines, and in return we provided Cobra gunships, fast patrol boats and, of course, our good selves. It was an arrangement that worked real well for us, as the Royal Marines are 'fucking A 1 guys' who know their shit and know how to fight, if you get my drift. Why they are not classed as Special Forces is beyond my comprehension, as they are each worth ten men. Well, that's my opinion. The only gripe I had working with them was the fact that they always seemed to lack suitable equipment for their mission, a good example being a severe lack of heavy weaponry for a start. For instance they had no automatic grenade launchers, nor indeed anywhere near enough ammo for their machine guns - something that is real basic. I have to admit to being a little shocked at their craft, as all they had out here were rigid raiders, landing craft and hovercraft, which were really not up to the task we were undertaking.

'To their credit they never complained about it, as they see themselves as raiders and not assaulters, and anyway they had us. I don't really want to harp on about this equipment issue as it's up to the British how they do things but I will say this. My uncle fought with British Commandos during World War II, and he really rated them but guess what his gripe was with them? You guessed it, lack of equipment!!! So, Mr Tony Blair, if you ever get to read this the message is simple, give your guys the right tools for the job. Anyway that's my bitching over for my Royal Marine friends and now to the business

Royal Marines and US Marines working together on a joint operation in southern Iraq. The professionalism of the Royal Marine Commandos, impressed the US Navy Seals who worked alongside them.

itself.

'Essentially, our role supporting the Royal Marines kept us pretty much down in the south of Iraq for most of the war, although I later went up country after Iraqi Freedom ended. Although we never really engaged the Iraqis in any serious firefight so to speak, we still had a few interesting experiences..

'On one occasion we were moving up a waterway towards Basra, when we came across a small building that was too small to be a house, yet too big to be a shelter, but it got our attention anyhow, due to the enormous amount of footprints that were around it.Why, we asked, does an insignificant building like this have so many visitors, especially those that wear military style footwear? To answer the question we mounted an extensive search operation in the vicinity of the building, both on the bank that the building was on, and the one on the other side of the waterway, as we suspected the presence of an underground facility. As we moved slowly towards the building, the Royal Marines took up position behind us - in effect they were the cavalry should things go wrong. My partner in crime jumped out of the boat first, while we provided cover by means of the 'Fifty' and the Mk 19. As he slowly moved up the bank to the left of the building, I jumped out of the boat and moved right, performing what was in effect a pincer movement. For a few seconds it was pretty tense, but once we were happy that nobody was at home, we relaxed and had a mosey around but found nothing incriminating. We eventually put the footprints down to the fact that this may have been a crossing point before the outbreak of hostilities, as this seemed a logical explanation.

'One day we decided to push further north, as we were simply finding no trade down here to speak of and things were becoming a tad tedious. On board our boat we had a small micro UAV, which we

made great use of, as it enabled us to survey the area in front of our line of advance. The Brits often teased us about this gizmo, as they had seen nothing like it before - but I never let them use it as I had signed it out - and I didn't want to have to pay for it if they crashed it - well that's my story. On one patrol however, it came in real useful when it spotted a number of abandoned Iraqi gunboats that had been tied up together close to a

A US Marine gunboat patrols the waterways inside Iraq, a scene reminiscent of Vietnam thirty years before.

fork in the waterways. From the distance these suckers looked like rust - buckets, but yet they still had weaponry onboard that looked remarkably serviceable - especially the radar controlled quad cannons that each mounted. After satisfying ourselves that everything was hunky - dory, we boarded them and carried out a thorough search operation - that again yielded nothing. While on board the boats, our Royal Marine friends decided that the rockets and munitions that were everywhere on the deck and below, needed to be dumped as they still could be used against us. Not wanting to be difficult with them, I helped them throw the main bulk of the weapons into the water - which prompted one of them to joke about 'Green Peace', and how they would react to such a move. Finally, after we were done here we came across yet another boat, which looked like a Staten Island ferry tug but

Royal Marines use a Rigid Raider boat to board an Iraqi vessel in search of weapons.

again yielded nothing. By now we are starting to feel like the crew of the PBR in the Vietnam film Apocalypse Now *- but minus the action. My personal opinion for this lack of action stems from the fact that we were just too big a force to take on - especially if you wanted to live afterwards. Yes, there were occasional pot-shots, but nothing more serious. Ironically, the biggest firefight of my tenure with the Royal Marines arose out of a Blue on Blue incident that no SEALS were involved in - the result being one Marine KIA, and several wounded. When I heard what had happened, it left a bad taste in my mouth - as potential incidents like these are always on your mind. And no matter how careful you are, it can happen - it just hurts more when they are guys that you know and respect.*

'From a personal perspective, my time on Al-Faw was interesting, albeit uneventful from a combat point of view - but I guess if we had not been there, then things may have been a darned sight hotter for everyone else concerned'.

AUSTRALIA - SPECIAL AIR SERVICE REGIMENT

Essentially, the SASR draws upon the best of British and American Special Forces doctrine and combines and adapts it to fit Australian military requirements, which are in many areas unique.

During Operation Iraqi Freedom in 2003, the SASR deployed with specialist troops from the newly established Incident Response Regiment (IRR) based at Holsworthy, New South Wales. Their mission: to combat Iraq's Weapons of Mass Destruction (WMD).

Other roles included direct support of Australia's quick reaction support force - 4RAR Commando unit, covert reconnaissance, hit and run operations and deep strike.

An Australian operator from 4RAR calls up the rest of his section after carrying out a close target reconnaisance. Note his weapon is an M16A2 rather than the normal issue Austeyr.

ISRAEL - CAESAREA

Israel's Caesarea is a special operations hit squad tasked with the elimination of commanders, controllers and financiers of Israel's enemies abroad. Although disbanded some years ago after a failed assassination attempt on Hamas leader, Khaled Masha'al, the unit was reactivated again in September 2002, following a serious upsurge in violence against Israeli citizens and members of its armed forces by Palestinian terrorists, belonging to the terrorist groups Islamic Jihad and Hamas.

Palestinian terrorists open fire on Israeli soldiers.

Despite almost two years of perpetual violence, in which hundreds of Israelis were either killed or injured by suicide bombers, the cycle of death continued, leaving the Israeli government and its security advisors with no choice but to take drastic action against the terrorists and their supporters.

Caesarea is currently headed by former army commando and agent, Meir Dagan, who operates under the command and control of the Israeli intelligence service, Mossad.

According to Mossad, Islamic extremists living abroad will become as vulnerable to attack as those killed by the IDF in the West Bank and Gaza, and with Mossad's reputation that is likely to be the case.

Caesarea comprises thirty highly trained fighters that are the elite of the elite within the Israeli security services. The squad is generally made up of former

Israeli Commandos in action. Caesarea are the elite of the elite and comprise generally Commandos who are fluent in other languages.

commandos that are fluent in at least one foreign language and have the ability to blend into new environments without attracting attention. For security reasons their faces are never shown, even to other Mossad agents, and many of them live as 'sleepers' in foreign countries. For many Caesarea agents serving out their tour of duty, years can pass by without any mission, but once activated their reactions are immediate and precise.

As selection criteria for joining Mossad is extremely demanding, with only one applicant in 1,000 receiving an employment offer, it comes as little surprise that within this already elite group only one candidate in 100 will make a Caesarea operative. Once deployed on operations and regardless of the numbers involved, only the best Caesarea agent within the hit squad will be allowed to carry out the hit.

Although much of Caesarea's operational history is highly classified, they are known to have killed the Palestinian terrorists responsible for the murder of eleven Israeli athletes during the 1972 Munich Olympics, with further operations sanctioned in Lebanon, Syria and Iraq.

Caesarea's mission statement is very simple: whatever they can't kill they close down.

POLAND - GROM

During Operation Iraqi Freedom, GROM operatives played a key role in supporting the allied forces efforts both covertly and overtly. They worked primarily with the US Navy SEALs, British SBS and the Australian diving teams in and around the Iraqi deep water port of Umm Qasr, on the Al-Faw peninsula. Operations carried out included search and control missions, the boarding and searching of Iraqi vessels, anti-sniper missions, EOD, force protection missions, overt water patrols, covert water patrols, tactical reconnaissance and urban CQB missions.

Polish GROM operatives conduct a search and sweep operation in the port of Umm Qasr.

UK - PARACHUTE REGIMENT

Based at Colchester, the Parachute Regiment is an integral part of the UK's 16 Air Assault Brigade and provides most of its infantry component. The Regiment is made up of three battalions, 1, 2 & 3, two of which are always assigned to the Brigade's air assault infantry.

In comparison with other countries that have a long history of parachute based operations such as Russia, Germany and Italy, Britain was slow to realize the potential of Airborne Forces and only formed a capability in 1940. However once a unit was formed, volunteers from the existing commando forces soon came forward leading to the formation of the 2 Airborne Brigade.

The first action fought by the Paras was in Tunisia (although they were not airdropped) where they earned from the Germans the nickname of *Die Roten Teufel* (The Red Devils, a name that they still have). By 1943, the Brigade had grown considerably in size and capability and now had its own glider borne force. Following a change of name to the 1st Airborne Division the Paras were dropped into Sicily wearing their 'Pegasus' airborne insignia and Red Berets, which was to be a precursor for the ambitious but ill-fated Operation Market Garden, where the Paras fought a valiant action at Arnhem, Holland in September 1944. As these events were taking place, a new formation known as the 6th Airborne Division was preparing for the D-Day invasion of Normandy.

After the war ended the Paras found themselves involved in numerous conflicts and internal security operations in Palestine, Malaya, Suez, Aden,

Four men of the 6th Airborne Division, the Parachute regiment, re-set watches prior to being dropped into Normandy during the D-Day invasion 1944.

Paras man a heavily armed Land Rover during a work up exercise in the UK.

A member of the Parachute regiment shows off the varied equipment and ammunition used by the soldiers of this elite force.

Borneo and Northern Ireland, culminating in the Falklands War in 1982.

In 1999, the Paras led the way into Kosovo for NATO and also participated in a spectacular hostage rescue operation in Sierra Leone. On their return to the UK they were permanently assigned to the newly formed 16 Air Assault Brigade in which they are a key component of its unique capabilities; however following the events of 11 September 2001 a small force was sent to Afghanistan as part of an international peacekeeping force, but did not involve 16 AAB.

All officers and men of the Parachute Regiment are volunteers and have to attend a rigorous two-day pre-selection course before attempting the feared recruit training course. The course lasts for some twenty-three weeks, with the first eight concentrating on basic military training which covers drill, weapons handling, field craft etc. After that the recruits spend some time on leadership training, rock-climbing, canoeing, abseiling etc. and then it's the big one, 'P Company' (Pre-Parachute Selection Company). This part of the course is

Airborne soldiers from 1 Para use an 81mm mortar to suppress enemy positions in Iraq.

the most physically demanding and is comparable with that of the Royal Marines Commando course. For those thirty-five per cent that pass P Company, a basic parachuting course awaits them that is their final hurdle before being presented with their 'Parachute Wings'.

During Operation Telic in 2003, the Paras found themselves engaged in numerous missions throughout southern Iraq, most of which involved heavy fighting. Their ability to deploy quickly by helicopter to any potential hotspot with overwhelming firepower proved a lethal and effective combination that the Iraqis simply could not beat, especially as the Paras could fight by day and night without any degradation in their capability.

PARACHUTE REGIMENT WEAPONS

Include the SA-80 A2 assault rifle, M16A2 assault rifle with M203 40mm grenade launcher, SA-80 A2 LSW light support weapon, M249 Minimi light machine gun, GPMG medium machine gun, M2 .50 heavy machine gun, 81mm mortar, LAW 80 anti-tank missile, Milan anti-tank missile and Starstreak MANPADS.

The SA80 A2 British assault rifle. Fires 5.56 calibre rounds and is fitted with a 4x magnification SUSAT sight.

UK - PATHFINDER PLATOON

Based in Colchester is Britain's elite 16 Air Assault Brigade and its reconnaissance force, the Pathfinder Platoon. By any normal military criteria this unit would be deemed Special Forces but, in typical British understatement, it is classed only as an elite specialist unit. However, for the members of the Pathfinder Platoon this poses no problem as they view themselves as being expert in the art of covert reconnaissance only, and not as a fighting force. They are being unduly modest, as they are members of the Parachute Regiment, a unit that has a fearsome fighting reputation around the world, and in effect they are an elite within an elite. Their excellent skills make them obvious candidates for the SAS, and many view the Pathfinders as simply a stepping stone between the Parachute Regiment and the SAS.

Originally formed during the Second World War, the Pathfinder unit had the unenviable role of jumping ahead of the main force of paratroopers and securing a DZ (Drop Zone) for them. In September 1944, Pathfinders of the 21st Independent Company parachuted into Arnhem to find and secure a DZ for Operation Market Garden. Although their part of the operation was a complete success, the unit was disbanded after the end of the war.

In 1981, 2 Para recognized the need for a Pathfinder Platoon and set about creating a modern equivalent that would have more or less the same role as the original Pathfinders of the Second World War. Despite the fact that it was only platoon strength (sixteen men), the new unit was known in 2 Para as C Company, and effectively became the eyes and ears of the Regiment.

In 1982, 2 Para's Pathfinder Platoon was split up and reformed into two platoons, Recce Platoon and Patrol Platoon. The title of 'platoon' was somewhat ironic because the unit was now operating at company strength.

In 1985, the Pathfinder Platoon became part of 5 Airborne Brigade and took on additional operational roles which involved covert reconnaissance and sabotage. Again, the title 'platoon' was retained even though the unit was at company strength.

The Pathfinders played an important role in Kosovo in 1999, where they were tasked with identifying safe and secure landing zones for helicopters bringing in British spearhead Forces prior to the arrival of the main allied invasion force. In September 2000, the Pathfinders deployed to Sierra Leone and participated in a spectacular hostage rescue operation that involved 2 Para, the SAS and elements of the SBS. The rescue operation was sanctioned after a group of British peacekeeping soldiers were taken hostage by a group of drug crazed rebels, known locally as the West Side Boys. Although aspects of this operation still remain highly classified, the role of the Pathfinders was significant in that they identified suitable helicopter assault points for 2 Para and then provided fire support as they fast-roped on to the LZ. This was, in fact, the Pathfinder's

second combat action in Sierra Leone, as they were involved in a skirmish with rebels while on a peacekeeping mission in 1999. They were also deployed with 2 Para to Kabul, Afghanistan, in 2002 for a short peacekeeping operation.

The Pathfinders Platoon is now part of the newly formed 16 Air Assault brigade, and acts as the Brigade's advance force. Its operational roles include covert reconnaissance, the location and marking of drop zones, tactical landing zones and helicopter landing zones for subsequent air assault operations. After the main force has landed, the platoon takes on the role of tactical intelligence gathering and works very closely with the Brigade's HQ.

The selection of Pathfinder candidates is very similar to that of the SAS, with only the best passing through the rigorous assessment phase. New recruits to the Pathfinders have to be placed on a year's probation before they are officially accepted into the unit's ranks. Any soldier not already parachute qualified must attend the basic parachute training course at RAF Brize Norton. Once qualified the soldiers must undergo HALO training, with some going on to complete the more advanced HAHO course. The soldiers are then assigned to either Air or Mountain Platoon, where they will be posted to one of the five 4-man platoons. The essential difference between the two platoons is that all Air Platoon troops are both HALO and HAHO trained, while Mountain Platoon is only trained in HALO and specializes in Arctic warfare.

Being a Para can be demanding but serving as a Pathfinder is something else, as there is a constant demand on each soldier to both maintain and acquire new skills. Soldiers learn survival and E & E techniques until they become second nature, as most of their time in conflict is going to be spent operating behind enemy lines. Although their prime mission is to operate covertly, if compromised they are trained to defend themselves in a truly devastating manner as each 4-man team carries two M249 Minimis, two M16 A2s, fitted with M203 grenade launchers, and copious amounts of hand grenades.

Members of the Pathfinder Platoon of 16 Air Assault Brigade offload an armed Land Rover.

Soldiers serving in the Pathfinders are expected to complete at least three years' service, with the option of a further extension, while officers only serve for two years. The idea behind these short service postings relates to the fact that both the officers and soldiers have a chance to share their knowledge and experience with other units and regiments.

The Pathfinders have links with many foreign units including the Jordanian Special Forces, US Army Rangers, US 82nd Airborne Pathfinders and the 2nd REP, French Foreign Legion.

During the initial phase of military operations in Iraq, the Pathfinders operated as a tactical recce force, providing intelligence on landing zones, enemy defensive positions and safe infiltration routes. However, towards the end of the war, their role changed to that of carrying out both recce and fighting patrols near the Iranian border, as there were fears of Iranian militants infiltrating Iraq for the purpose of encouraging insurrection among the Sunni population.

Other missions carried out during this period, included Northern Ireland style 'eagle patrols' and 'sweep and clear' operations near the Rumailah oil fields as these were being targeted by elements of the Fedayeen Saddam and 'The Return.'

PATHFINDERS PLATOON WEAPONS

Equipment used by the Pathfinders Platoon includes state-of-the-art GPS and NVG systems, portable satellite communications, Land-Rover 110 SOVs, Land Rover 90s, Quad Bikes and Argocat ATVs. The Pathfinders make extensive use of the Land-Rovers for long range recce patrols and greatly value their ability to carry a large variety of weapons such as the GPMG, Mk-19 40mm automatic grenade launcher and Browning .50 heavy machine gun. Weapons used include the M16 A2 with M203 grenade launcher, M249 Minimi, 7.62 GPMG, Browning HP, Colt Commando and SA-80 A2.

For HALO operations the Pathfinders use the GQ360 Ram Air Parachute as it gives them a greater amount of control and features an automatic chute deployment device which opens the parachute at a preset altitude using the Hitefinder opening instrument. The standard height for HALO jumps to commence is 25,000 feet with the parachute set to deploy at around 2,500 feet. These heights offer the aircraft protection from radar detection and also give the soldier a chance to deploy his reserve chute in the event of a failure, or Roman Candle as the Pathfinders would say. For HAHO missions the soldier needs to jump with oxygen as his jump and chute deployment height is 30,000 feet. This height allows the soldier to glide for almost ninety minutes before hitting the ground. In good wind conditions a soldier can glide for a considerable distance which reduces the chances of radar detection for both him and the insertion aircraft. Pathfinders wear standard British Army combat uniforms but tend to wear either Para or SAS smocks depending on personal preference. They also wear the famous Para Red Beret with its distinctive cap badge.

The GPMG (General Purpose Machine Gun). Uses 7.62 calibre bullets and is an effective long range support weapon.

UK - SAS OPERATIONS 1958-2003.

Date: 1958-59
Location: Jebel Akhdar, Oman
Operation: Two SAS Squadrons are deployed to Oman to put down a rebellion on the formidable natural fortress of the Jebel Akhdar.

Date: 1963-66
Location: Borneo
Operation: The SAS finds itself back in the jungle fighting Indonesian forces and rebel guerrillas who are opposed to the formation of the Federation of Malaysia.

Date: 1964-67

Location: Aden
Operation: SAS operations are mounted in the Radfan area against tribesmen and guerrillas. These were known as 'Keeni-Meeni' operations.

Date: 1969-94
Location: Northern Ireland
Operation: SAS are sent to Northern Ireland to support the British Army and the Royal Ulster Constabulary (RUC) by mounting intelligence gathering and anti-terrorist operations against the IRA and its supporters.

An SAS trooper patrolling under the dense canopy of the Borneo jungle during the 1960s.

Numerous operations were mounted during this period that resulted in both SAS and IRA fatalities. The most successful operation of this campaign was the ambush of IRA terrorists at Loughall that resulted in the complete annihilation of their East Tyrone Brigade.

Date: 1970-76
Location: Oman
Operation: SAS is sent to Oman, to defeat communist guerrillas attempting to overthrow the government of Oman. This particular operation featured a highly successful 'hearts and minds' campaign that persuaded other Omanis not to join in the insurgency.

Date: 1980
Location: London
Operation: The SAS carried out one of its most spectacular operations under the gaze of the world's media and brought them instant worldwide recognition. Operation Nimrod was launched to either kill or capture terrorists that were holding hostages in the Iranian Embassy in London and is now viewed as a text-book example of how to execute a hostage rescue mission.

Date: 1981
Location: Gambia
Operation: SAS helps to restore President Jawara to power in the Gambia after a coup.

Date: 1982
Location: Falkland Islands
Operation: The SAS are deployed to the Falkland Islands to carry out intelligence and raiding operations against

London 1980. The SAS are brought into the public eye, following their appearance on the news during the Iranian Embassy Siege.

Argentinian forces that were occupying the island illegally. Although there were many significant missions undertaken, the key operations during this conflict were the retaking of Grytviken, South Georgia, and the Pebble Island raid. The SAS were highly successful during this war but regrettably lost eighteen men in a non-combat related helicopter crash.

The Falklands 1982. SAS troopers are rescued after their helicopter came down in South Georgia during a white out.

Date: 1989
Location: Columbia
Operation: 22 SAS is deployed to Columbia, to take part in the anti-cocaine war after the British government received a request for military assistance. This included training for the Columbian forces and missions against the drug barons.

Date: 1990-91
Location: The Gulf
Operation: The SAS is deployed to the Gulf, in support of the UN-led campaign to remove Iraqi forces from Kuwait. The Regiment found itself operating primarily in Iraq on missions against the Iraqis' Scud missiles and their support infrastructure. They were highly successful and operated in ways very similar to the original SAS in North Africa.

The Gulf War 1990-1991. SAS mobility patrols search for Scud launchers.

Date: 1994-95
Location: Bosnia
Operation: SAS teams were deployed to Bosnia in small numbers to gain intelligence on the Serbian forces and to provide target designation for RAF strike aircraft.

Date: 1997
Location: Peru
Operation: Six-man SAS team sent to Lima, Peru, following the takeover of the Japanese Ambassador's residence in January 1997 along with operators from the US Delta Force.

Date: 1998
Location: The Gulf
Operation: In February 1998 the SAS deployed a squadron to the Gulf when Saddam Hussein threatened to start another war. They were tasked with reconnaissance missions and the rescue of downed pilots.

Date: 1998
Location: Albania
Operation: In March 1998, a 4-man team was deployed to Albania, to rescue a British aid worker named Robert Welch. The team located him and secured his rescue by driving to the coast using Land-Rovers. Upon arrival they were met by two helicopters. One provided a security force at the RV point, while the other extracted the rescue team and their vehicles.

Date: 1999
Location: Kosovo
Operation: Following the invasion of Kosovo by Serbian forces, the SAS were deployed to assist in finding targets for NATO aircraft and to rescue downed aircrew. They also provided support to the Kosovo Liberation Army (KLA) and helped in the apprehension of Serbian war criminals.

An SAS patrol in Sierra Leone 2000.

Date: 2000
Location: Sierra Leone
Operation: The SAS were initially called in to provide an overt presence in Sierra Leone, in support of a UN peacekeeping effort. However, a number of British soldiers were captured and held hostage by a ruthless militia, known as the West Side Boys. In response the SAS launched a spectacular rescue operation in conjunction with 1 Para and secured the release of the hostages for the tragic loss of one soldier.

Date: 2001
Location: Afghanistan
Operation: Following the terrorist attack on the US on 11 September 2001, the SAS were deployed to Afghanistan in support of UK operations against terrorism. The SAS carried out recce and targeting missions for US forces against Taliban and Al-Qaeda soldiers and their equipment. In addition they also provided support to the Northern Alliance and helped in finding safe areas for the delivery of humanitarian aid. They

Afghanistan 2001. SAS troopers search for Al-Qaeda soldiers.

played a key role in this war and were extremely successful in operating in very difficult and demanding conditions.

THE SAS

On 2 August 1990 Iraqi forces invaded Kuwait. Realizing that if he failed to react Saudi Arabia might also be invaded, President George Bush initiated Operation Desert Shield. With the support of the UN an international force was sent to the Gulf to retake Kuwait in an operation that was called Desert Storm.

Under the aegis of Special Operations Command (SOCOM), based in Tampa, Florida, the United States provided the main contribution of Special Forces personnel, closely followed by the UK. The French also sent over a significant contingent of their Foreign Legion and 6th Parachute Division, while Australia and New Zealand provided a combined ANZAC SAS Squadron. Recognizing the key role that Special Forces had played during the Falklands War, the UK sent almost the entire regular SAS Regiment to the region, a force that amounted to some 700 men. It was made up from A, B and D squadrons, plus fifteen reservist volunteers from R Squadron. G Squadron was committed to other operations, including counter-terrorist duties back in the UK, and was not deployed to the Gulf. In support of the SAS, members of the Royal Marines, Special Boat Service (SBS) were deployed to the region, along with RAF special operations aircrew. Clearly, for the UK this was a major operation, and the coalition would later express how greatly it valued the participation of the SAS in support of its mission.

HUMAN SHIELDS

As the coalition forces gathered together in Saudi Arabia for the forthcoming operation, there was a serious and troubling development. Having anticipated a response from the West, Saddam Hussein had been busy placing hostages, who had been captured at the outbreak of the conflict, around likely military targets. In effect, he had turned these people into human shields.

The American forces, led by General Schwarzkopf, and the British, led by General de la Billiere, wasted no time in planning a rescue mission for their respective national hostages. There was, however, a major obstacle in their way: the hostages had been positioned around numerous sites, meaning that to coordinate simultaneous attacks on all of them would have been impossible. The coalition leaders were quick to realize that even if some of the hostages could be rescued by the SAS and Delta, it was fair to assume that the others would be executed in reprisal. The risks were just too great to contemplate such a mission. As the SAS tentatively considered their options, the hostage crisis suddenly came to

Above: General Schwarzkopf.

Below: General de la Billière

an end. Saddam decided to release the hostages as a gesture of goodwill, following intense international political pressure. This was to be just the first of many mind games that he would play during the conflict, but for now the SAS was relieved to be able to get on with planning other missions that would, it hoped, bring about a swift conclusion to the Gulf crisis.

General Sir Peter de la Billiere, the joint British Commander-in-Chief in the Gulf was a veteran of the SAS, and knew their value. This was to be of key importance in convincing General Norman Schwarzkopf, the Commander of the coalition ground forces, that the SAS could play a major part in this operation if given permission to operate behind Iraqi front lines.

General Schwarzkopf was initially sceptical of the potential of the SAS to operate behind enemy lines in the way that was at first put forward. However he was impressed with their track record and gave permission for two squadrons to be deployed on 20 January 1991.

The SAS wasted no time in infiltrating Iraqi territory. Within hours of their deployment they were driving around deep behind enemy lines looking for targets of opportunity. In many ways they were performing like the Long Range Desert Group LRDG of the Second World War, the forefathers of the SAS. A and D Squadrons had been divided into mobile fighting columns, each of which had eight Land-Rover 110s, armed with Browning 0.5in heavy machine guns. In addition to the primary armament, they carried other weapons such as 7.62mm GPMGs, 40mm Mk 19 grenade launchers and Milan anti-tank missiles. The SAS was particularly impressed with the Milan, as its thermal imaging sight provided the ability for them to operate in total darkness. It could provide imagery out to a range of 8 kilometres (five miles). However the missile itself was limited to a range of 2,000 metres (6,555 feet) on account of it being wire-guided.

Each column also had a Unimog utility vehicle which carried the bulk of the extra stores needed for long range operations. Typically this consisted of fuel, rations, ammunition, vehicle spares and nuclear, biological and chemical (NBC)

An SAS column of Land Rovers prepares to cross the border in Iraq. They were to return to their original role of fighting in the desert, as they did in the Second World War.

A Unimog utility vehicle drives off in support of an SAS mobility patrol.

SAS troopers, armed with the M16 M203 combination - a lethal mixture.

equipment. A number of motorbikes also accompanied each column; these provided a scout capability to the front and side flanks.

Before embarking for Iraq, the SAS had been training in the United Arab Emirates honing their skills for what was to come. During this training they decided not to take their Light Strike Vehicles (LSV) with them into Iraq. This dune buggy like vehicle could carry massive firepower over rough terrain very quickly; however they were not as reliable as the Land-Rover 110s and suffered from problems with their centre of gravity once loaded up with equipment.

On average each mobility column had thirty SAS troops assigned to it with their own personal weapons. Most carried an M16 assault rifle fitted with a 40mm M203 grenade launcher, along with a small pistol for personal protection. The firepower each mobility column possessed was truly awesome and this gave the SAS a major advantage over the enemy in the event of a contact. For navigation, the SAS had Global Positioning Systems (GPS), compasses and, in some cases, sextants. They also carried secure state-of-the-art communication systems to enable them to receive orders and to relay information back to their command centre as required.

Each mobility column was tasked with a different area of responsibility within a region. Some of these extended almost 400 kilometres (250 miles) behind enemy lines. The SAS generally operated at night, taking full advantage of the hours of darkness as the Iraqi forces had very little night vision capability at troop level. During the hours of daylight the SAS would lay-up in whatever cover was available, be it a wadi or a sunken feature in what was generally a flat landscape.

The terrain in western Iraq was mainly lava bed, mixed with wadis that proved to be hard going for the mobility columns, but this problem also hampered Iraqi movements as well. The SAS spaced their vehicles out as much as possible when driving to prevent enemy ambushes. On occasions the spread of these vehicles could be as much as one kilometre making it very difficult for an Iraqi force to hit them all during an attack.

One major advantage that the SAS had over the Iraqi forces was that they were setting the agenda. The Iraqi soldiers simply never knew when or where the SAS would strike, and as a result their morale plummeted.

On one occasion a recce unit for an Iraqi artillery brigade stumbled onto an SAS position. Thinking they were friendly forces, the Iraqi soldiers stopped their Russian built Gaz-69 truck near to the SAS unit. An Iraqi officer carrying a map case got out of the vehicle and proceeded to walk towards the SAS soldiers. As he got closer he realized his mistake and pulled out a pistol. The SAS patrol had no choice but to open fire and in the subsequent firefight all except one of the Iraqi soldiers were killed. The surviving Iraqi soldier was taken prisoner and flown back to Saudi Arabia for interrogation, along with maps and plans that the SAS had discovered in his vehicle. The SAS gained good intelligence from this patrol and were able to identify further high value targets that had not been detected previously by air assets.

The biggest problem the SAS faced was the weather rather than the enemy. Intelligence had failed to brief them on the severity of the cold in this region. As a result the SAS soldiers only carried lightweight smocks that were totally unsuitable for these conditions. As an interim solution, Arab blanket coats were procured in the region, along with gloves and local headdress. These items were then issued during routine re-supply drops made by the RAF, using Chinook helicopters.

As the SAS continued operations behind Iraqi lines, several priority missions were tasked to them. Military planners in Riyadh needed to know if the ground in Iraq could support the weight of tanks and heavy vehicles, so samples were

The SAS operated primarily at night and laid up in wadis or sunken features during the day as it minimized their exposure.

Looking for Scuds. The SAS operated deep behind enemy lines, causing chaos and confusion amongst the Iraqi army.

required before any major ground war could begin. The SAS carried out this mission with great success and the results proved to be invaluable to the coalition.

As the missions intensified, the SAS realized that the Achilles heel of the Iraqis' war machine was their communication network. This consisted of fibre optic cables buried underground that were difficult to find from the air but could easily be destroyed by small teams on the ground. The SAS employed two tactics against them. They would first blow up some of the cables with hand placed charges. They would then leave booby traps for the Iraqi repair teams, so that they would be forced to take their time finding any devices that had been hidden in or around the optic cables. This time factor was critical to the coalition forces, because the longer the SAS kept the Iraqi forces in the dark about what was going on around the battlefield, the easier it would be for conventional military forces to operate.

On one particular operation, the SAS were tasked with destroying a communications tower deep behind Iraqi lines. They attacked at night using their heavy vehicle mounted weapons and succeeded in destroying the tower and all of its support equipment. The SAS patrol that carried out the attack was somewhat surprised at how little resistance there was during the firefight. They later found out that the Iraqi soldiers had been under the impression that they were being attacked from the air and had taken shelter in their underground bunkers. This was to be a common occurrence because the Iraqis at this time had no idea that the SAS were operating in such a mobile way so deep within their lines.

The SAS were causing absolute chaos behind the Iraqi lines, and this forced the Iraqi commanders to withdraw front line troops from their duties and redeploy them in defensive roles around their rear echelon areas. The SAS tactics of cutting roads and creating diversions was clearly paying off in this war, and mixed with coordinated air operations, the effect was devastating.

On 24 January 1991 the role of the SAS was changed to that of anti-Scud missile operations and this remained the case for the rest of the war. The sudden reason for this change in role for the SAS was brought about by an attack on Israel with Iraqi Scud missiles on the night of 18 January 1991. It suddenly became apparent to the coalition that if these attacks continued against Israel

Somewhere in Iraq. An SAS soldier brews up next to his Land Rover.

there was a real danger that Israel would enter the conflict in retaliation, which would have resulted in most of the Arab contingents leaving the coalition. General Schwarzkopf quickly realized the implications of these Scud attacks and ordered a maximum effort against both the Scuds and their launch sites.

Western Intelligence agencies were well aware of the fact that Iraq had a great number of these surface-to-surface missiles and had launched over 200 alone against Iran in 1988. They knew that Iraq had received over 800 Scuds from the Soviets in the early 1980s and that a number of them had been modified to carry chemical warheads. This capability caused great concern to the coalition because they knew that Saddam Hussein had used chemical weapons against his own people without any hesitation, and that he had both the method and means of delivering them into Israel or any other country that fell within range of his launch sites.

It was estimated that Iraq had twenty-eight static launch sites and around thirty-six mobile launchers, which were mounted on large 8-wheeled vehicles that required a number of other support units to enable their operation. At first the coalition felt that this threat could be eliminated by air power alone. However they found the Scuds very difficult to locate from the air and, even when they were successful in finding them, the time taken to put an air strike together was too long. In many cases they arrived after the Scuds had departed.

The SAS knew that the Scuds were the key issue of the war for the coalition and that their destruction was paramount to ensure victory over the Iraqis. Never a unit to do anything half-heartedly, the SAS decided to attack the Scud threat in three ways.

First, they would deploy road-watch patrols to report on Scud movements. Second, the mobility columns that had proved so successful at the start of the conflict would be used to attack the Scud convoys at every opportunity that presented itself.

A Scud missile about to be launched from its transporter. Scuds proved very hard to locate and new tactics had to be developed in order to destroy them.

Third, SAS units would intensify their operations against the Iraqis underground communications network, as this was the principle means of issuing orders to the Scud units from Baghdad.

The road-watch patrols were supplied by B Squadron and were made up of three 8- man teams who were tasked with observing the Iraqis' three main supply routes (MSRs) that ran from the Euphrates valley to the Jordanian border. The teams were called the north, central and south road-watch teams and were inserted into western Iraq by RAF Chinooks on 22 January.

Up until this point things had been going pretty well for the SAS, however everything was about to change for the worst. Before the three road-watch teams were inserted there had been some problems with the supply of various items of kit for this mission, as the other squadrons had taken the majority of the stores with them on their anti-Scud patrols. As a result B Squadron was short of several key items such as grenades for its M203 grenade launchers. There was also a problem with the maps. Intelligence only had pilots' charts available and these only showed basic land features in a very small scale that was of little use to a soldier planning a mission.

SAS soldiers, by the sheer nature of their character, are not quitters, so despite the setbacks, they decided to go ahead with the road-watch missions and just tough it out. On the way to their respective drop-off points (DOPs) they landed at a US forward operating base (FOB) to take on extra fuel for their RAF Chinook helicopters. While on the ground they scrounged some extra ammunition and rations for their mission from the American ground personnel who were refuelling their helicopters and, although they were allies, nothing was discussed regarding their final destination. Each SAS team operated separately from the other and no details were exchanged regarding where they were being dropped off or at what time. It was a strictly need-to-know operation and as standard operating procedure (SOP) only the mission planners would know where each team was to operate.

Within hours of being inserted into Iraq there were problems. There simply was no practical cover for the teams to lay-up during the day and the proposed operating areas were crawling with Iraqi soldiers and, in some cases, civilians. This problem with the terrain also caused setbacks for the US Special Forces and in one case an A-Team had to be extracted in a spectacular manner while receiving heavy enemy fire.

For two of the SAS teams, south and central respectively, the ground situation was totally unacceptable for them to be able to operate in a covert manner for any length of time and the risk of being compromised was just too great. After carefully considering their options they decided to abort their missions and return to base. One team returned in the Chinook that had brought them, while the other walked back to Saudi Arabia, a distance of some 200 kilometres. There were a few raised eyebrows regarding the two aborted missions. In one case the section commander of one of them was virtually accused of being a coward, while the other was given a pat on the back for calling in an air strike on two mobile Iraqi radar systems that were located near to them. As the fate of the other team became known, the section commanders' decisions were seen to have been correct as their first duty is to the men under their command and not the mission.

The story of the team that remained behind was to become a legend in modern warfare. Northern road watch team or 'Bravo Two Zero' as they were codenamed decided to stay in Iraq and perform their mission as best as they could under the circumstances. Only hours into their mission and there were serious issues for them. The place where they were laying-up was near to an Iraqi encampment and, to make matters worse, they were faced with every soldier's worst nightmare. A young Iraqi boy had spotted the SAS team, and they now faced a dreadful decision. Either kill the boy and get away themselves or let him live and face the consequences of the Iraqi army being alerted to their presence. SAS soldiers are men of great honour and do not wage war against

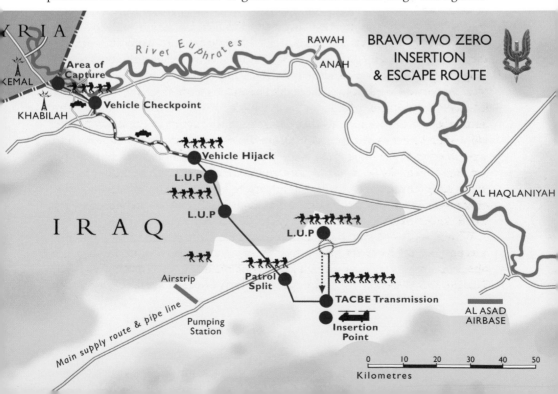

The most famous SAS patrol of Operation Desert Storm, Bravo Two Zero, whose Escape and Evasion became an SAS legend.

civilians. The choice had been made: they were going to take their chances and make a run for it, as he 'who fights and runs away, lives to fight another day'.

With the alarm raised the Iraqis were on the trail of the SAS team very quickly, and they had little choice but to escape and evade capture by putting some distance between them and the Iraqi patrols. They decided to make for Syria as it offered them the best chance of survival. There was little hope of them being extracted by helicopter. Under the command of Sergeant Andy McNab the team tabbed at a frantic pace to keep ahead of the Iraqis. They had one comfort in the fact that the coalition had total air supremacy and there was little chance of Iraqi helicopters being sent in to search for them. As the SAS soldiers crossed the Arabian Desert, fate played a dreadful card. The weather conditions were appalling and the soldiers had to battle through a lethal cocktail of rain, sleet, driving wind and snow. Even with warm clothing this would have been a challenge, but these men were only wearing lightweight smocks as they had been forced to ditch their spare kit in order to make better progress. In an effort to increase their overall chances of survival, the team decided to split up into two groups. As they pushed themselves to the edge of exhaustion one soldier, Sergeant Vince Phillips, became separated from his group and died of hypothermia. The other members of his team tried in vain to find him but due to the driving sleet in which they were caught up, this proved impossible. Their luck was about to run out as well as they found themselves surrounded by Iraqi soldiers. One was forced to surrender while the other made a spectacular escape. Walking day and night he covered over 200 kilometres on foot and made it to the Syrian border. If ever there was an example of what gives a man the right to wear the SAS beret then this was it. For the last two days of this soldier's journey he had no water and yet he still carried on and at no time ever considered giving up.

The other five members of the team made it to a town called Al Qaim, near the Jordanian border, where their luck finally ran out. Having fought their way through many firefights on the way they bumped into a large group of Iraqi soldiers and all hell broke loose. Although heavily outnumbered they fought a

> 'He who fights and runs away, lives to fight another day'.

series of running battles and inflicted heavy casualties on the Iraqis as they tried to shake them off. One of the SAS soldiers, Trooper Robert Consiglio, was killed as he covered the withdrawal of his team and soon after a further two were captured after running out of ammunition. Amazingly the remaining two members of the team avoided capture and found shelter in a small cabin, but tragedy struck. One of the soldiers Lance Corporal Lane, collapsed and later died of hypothermia. The other soldier, who had been with him, tried to escape but was captured as he fled towards the border, marking the end of SAS team 'Bravo Two Zero'.

Although technically this mission failed to carry out its objectives as originally tasked, it caused absolute chaos to the Iraqi forces and left over 250 of their soldiers dead and several hundred injured. The after effects of this mission rippled across Iraq and many more Iraqi units were withdrawn from the front line to search for any remaining SAS teams that were operating behind their lines.

Although the road-watch teams had been unable to gain intelligence on the Scuds' movements as originally planned, the destruction of the Scuds remained a top priority for the SAS. For the other squadrons operating behind Iraqi lines it was business as usual as they went about looking for mobile Scud units to attack in their designated operational areas. The SAS's operational area was based around the Iraqi H-2 airfield, an area some thirty-two kilometres (twenty miles) long by twenty-six kilometres (seventeen miles) wide and was designated the 'Southern Scud Box'. The SAS however, called it 'Scud Alley'.

American Special Forces worked very closely with the SAS, and were responsible for the 'Northern Scud Box', based around Al Qaim. Like the SAS they created their own nickname for their operational area. To them it was 'Scud Boulevard'.

Within days of crossing the border into Iraq, one of the SAS mobility columns discovered a camouflaged Scud site that was about to launch a salvo of missiles against Israel. They knew that they had to act quickly so they called in an air strike. Within minutes of their request USAF strike aircraft hit the site and completely destroyed it. The SAS wasted no time in departing from the scene, because there were very real concerns that some of the Scud missiles might have chemical warheads containing nerve agents such as Sarin, which the Iraqis had used against the Iranians.

The SAS were also very aware of the fact that the Iraqis had patrols out looking for them so they needed to be constantly vigilant. Whenever they stopped to refuel or rearm they would form a defensive circle using the vehicles for protection against any possible attack. On one occasion this tactic paid off, as an SAS mobility column found itself under attack from a larger Iraqi force. A fierce firefight ensued and eventually the Iraqis withdrew after taking a number of casualties and losing three of their vehicles from heavy machine-gun fire.

The SAS concentrated their patrols around Wadi Amij, near the town of Ar Rutbah, as they found this area good for trade. On 3 February 1991, a mobility column from D Squadron spotted an Iraqi convoy of fourteen vehicles. Wasting no time the commander of the column called in an air strike and watched it being attacked by American F-15s and A-10s using rockets, bombs and cannon fire. The convoy was being cut to pieces by the ordnance and several vehicles exploded in a spectacular manner, yet amazingly a number of vehicles and their crews survived the attack and had to be engaged by the SAS ground force. Using their heavy machine guns and Milan anti-tank missiles they picked off the remaining vehicles; however, the Iraqi soldiers had now got into cover and were returning fire. The SAS called in another air strike to finish off the convoy and withdrew during its execution.

For the Iraqis, life was becoming very difficult and they were being forced to use more and more troops to protect their Scud convoys. This only made them larger targets. The continuous combination of air strikes and ground attacks was taking its toll on the Iraqi forces and the tide was now beginning to turn in the coalition's favour.

Although Scud Alley was the SAS's prime hunting ground for Scuds, not all encounters occurred there. On one particular mission, an SAS mobility column was having difficulty locating a suspected Scud launching site and couldn't contact its HQ for verification of the details. After three days of searching the suspected area, the commander of the column decided to return to his base over the allied border. As the vehicles sped through the barren flat desert they spotted a number of vehicles ahead of them. They closed to within 600 metres to identify the convoy and discovered that it was a mobile Scud launcher complete with support vehicles. The convoy had stopped and its soldiers were in the process of camouflaging their vehicles; however they had neglected to post any sentries. This was to prove a fatal mistake for them. The SAS soldiers quickly got into an attack formation and opened fire on the Iraqis with their Milan missiles. All of the Scud vehicles were hit and destroyed and the Iraqis were unable to fire on the SAS, because of the thick, acrid smoke being produced by the burning vehicles.

A fully armed American F-15 jet fighter. The SAS patrols were able to call upon fighters like these to knock out mobile Scud launchers.

The Chinook, work horse of the Special Forces in Iraq whose crews flew dangerous missions deep into enemy territory in order to insert SAS patrols.

On another occasion an SAS column spotted a large Scud site that was heavily protected by Iraqi troops in good defensive positions. The SAS commander felt that it would be a difficult target to attack without sustaining heavy losses and decided to call in an air strike. As the SAS column withdrew, a number of USAF F-15s flew over them and attacked the Scud site with cluster bombs and laser guided munitions. Under normal circumstances the SAS would have observed the strike and reported back on its effectiveness; however due to the large number of Iraqi forces in the area this was not possible. Some hours later the SAS commander was informed that the USAF had carried out a recce of the Scud site and discovered that some of the launchers and their missiles had survived the air strike and were still capable of operation. To be sure of their destruction they had to be attacked again, this time by the SAS.

The commander of the SAS mobility column agreed to attack the Scud site,

Three members of the Regiment, pose for the camera in front of a Union Jack. Because they were so deep behind enemy lines, these were often laid out in order to protect them from friendly fire air strikes.

but needed more men. HQ Squadron deployed a small team of SAS soldiers by helicopter to reinforce the mobility column and a hastily drawn-up plan was put together. The commander of the column decided to attack at dawn, but needed to draw the Iraqi soldiers out of their heavily defended encampment to give him a better chance of success against the remaining targets. With typical SAS ingenuity he ordered his men to place small charges about one kilometre from the Iraqi positions, the theory being that when they went off, the Iraqi troops would be lured out of their positions and the SAS would then take advantage of the confusion and commence their attack.

As dawn broke the next morning the charges exploded, but to the credit of the Iraqis they stayed put and were now on their guard and well prepared for an attack. They suddenly started firing wildly at any possible place were a vehicle or soldier could hide but hit nothing. They didn't have to wait very long for a response from the SAS. On a nearby ridge the SAS had formed up with their vehicles in a crescent shaped formation that allowed the maximum concentration of firepower to bear. They placed their Milan posts on the outside flanks along with the newly arrived reinforcements, while the machine gun equipped vehicles positioned themselves in the centre of the formation. As they opened fire all hell broke loose. The machine guns concentrated on the Iraqi soldiers defending the position, leaving the Milans to pick off the Scud launchers. One by one they exploded, sending massive fireballs into the air that could be seen for miles. The Iraqi forces were completely overwhelmed by the lethal concentration of firepower and sustained heavy casualties. Once the SAS commander was satisfied that every target of value had been destroyed, he ordered his men to withdraw.

Although the destruction of the Scud launchers remained paramount, the SAS still had to find and destroy any Iraqi facility that supported their operation. Both the SAS and SBS had mounted operations against the Iraqis' communication network in an attempt to starve them of information and this, in part, had been successful. However there still remained a number of facilities that were supporting the Scuds that had to be taken out. On 21 February 1991, A Squadron was involved in an attack on a communications facility that supported the Scuds operations. As they withdrew from the attack they came under intense enemy fire and an SAS motorcyclist, Lance Corporal David Denbury, was hit and fatally wounded. The SAS went on to fight further running battles with the Iraqis over the next few days; however it was becoming clear that the Iraqis could now no longer operate in Scud Alley without the risk of being attacked.

As a result of the intensive anti-Scud operations, the Iraqis started to withdraw their remaining mobile launchers deeper into Iraq for greater protection. The withdrawal meant that Iraq could now no longer target the Israelis as they were out of Scud range, but that didn't stop them from firing at Saudi Arabia which they continued to do right up until the end of the war.

For the SAS the Gulf War showed off this Regiment's unique capabilities in a spectacular manner and, in many cases, it showed just how little had changed since their original hit and run tactics were used in North Africa during the Second World War. One piece of equipment that proved to be highly effective for the SAS in the desert was the Global Positioning System (GPS). These small hand-held devices received information from orbiting satellites regarding their relative position and this enabled SAS teams to know exactly where they were at any given time. The devices were accurate to within a few metres. The benefits of such a system were enormous as they allowed SAS teams to call in air strikes with absolute precision and avoid any risk of collateral damage.

For the SAS the Gulf War provided them with a means of proving how a small team could cause chaos and destruction to a large army in a manner that was out of all proportion for the size of the force used. The SAS inflicted significant losses on the Iraqi army but paid a price for this victory. In all, four members of the SAS Regiment lost their lives; two from actual combat and two from the severe weather conditions that prevailed in the region.

SAS motorcyclist, Lance Corporal David Denbury who was hit and fatally wounded during a contact with an Iraqi patrol.

The Global Positioning System (GPS), which proved to be highly effective for the SAS, while operating in the desert.

Many people will recall the visible side of the Gulf War, the air strikes, the ground invasion but few really appreciate the unseen war that took place in 1991. It is no exaggeration to state that the SAS played a key role in this war and had they failed in their Scud busting missions, the result of the war could have been very different.

After the war was over it was revealed that the USAF, Special Operations Group (SOG), had launched a major operation to rescue the 'Bravo Two Zero' team. However they failed to find them as the frequencies of their radios were set to a different one to that of the SAS team, and they had no way of knowing where they were heading.

SECRET

United States Central Command
Office of the Commander-in-Chief Operation Desert Storm
APO New York 09852-0006

9 March 1991
To: Sir Patrick Hine
Air Chief Marshal
Joint Headquarters
Royal Air Force Wycombe
Buckinghamshire HP14 4U

Thru: Sir Peter de la Billiere
KCB, CBE, DSO, MC
Lieutenant General
British Forces Commander Middle East
Riyadh, Saudi Arabia

Subject: Letter of Commendation for the 22nd Special Air Service (SAS) Regiment

1. I wish to officially commend the 22nd Special Air Service (SAS) Regiment for their totally outstanding performance of military operations during Operation Desert Storm.

2. Shortly after the initiation of the strategic air campaign, it became apparent that the coalition forces would be unable to eliminate Iraq's firing of Scud missiles from western Iraq into Israel.

The continued firing of Scuds on Israel carried with it enormous unfavorable political ramifications and could, in fact, have resulted in the dismantling of the carefully crafted coalition. Such a dismantling would have adversely affected in ways difficult to measure the ultimate outcome of the military campaign. It became apparent that the only way that the coalition could succeed in reducing these Scud launches was by physically placing military forces on the ground in the vicinity of the western launch sites. At that time, the majority of available coalition forces were committed to the forthcoming military campaign in the eastern portion of the theatre of operations. Further, none of these forces possessed the requisite skills and abilities required to conduct such a dangerous operation. The only force deemed qualified for this critical mission was the 22nd Special Air Service (SAS) Regiment.

3. From the first day they were assigned their mission until the last day of the conflict, the performance of the 22nd Special Air Service (SAS) Regiment was courageous and highly professional. The area in which they were committed proved to contain far more numerous enemy forces than had been predicted by every intelligence estimate, the terrain was much more difficult than expected and the weather conditions were unseasonably brutal. Despite these hazards, in a very short period of time the 22nd Special Air Service (SAS) Regiment was successful in totally denying the central corridor of western Iraq Scud units. The result was that the principal areas used by the Iraqis to fire Scuds on Tel Aviv were no longer available to them. They were required to move their Scud missile firing forces to the northwest portion of Iraq and from that location the firing of Scud missiles was essentially militarily ineffective.

4. When it became necessary to introduce United States Special Operations Forces into the area to attempt to close down the northwest Scud areas, the 22nd Special Air Service (SAS) Regiment provided invaluable assistance to the U.S. forces. They took every possible measure to ensure the U.S. forces were thoroughly briefed and were able to profit from the valuable lessons that had been learned by earlier SAS deployments into western Iraq. I am completely convinced that had the U.S. forces not received these thorough indoctrinations by SAS personnel U.S. forces would have suffered a much higher rate of casualties than was ultimately the case. Further, the SAS and U.S. joint forces immediately merged into a combined fighting force where the synergetic effect of these fine units ultimately caused the enemy to be convinced that they were facing forces in western Iraq that were more than tenfold the size of those they were actually facing. As a result, large numbers of enemy forces that might otherwise have been deployed in the eastern theatre were tied down in western Iraq.

5. The performance of the 22nd Special Air Service (SAS) Regiment during Operation Desert Storm was in the highest traditions of the professional military service and in keeping with the proud history and tradition that had been established by that regiment. Please ensure that this commendation receives appropriate attention and is passed on to the unit and its members.

H. Norman Schwarzkopf
General, U.S. Army
Commander-in-Chief

It is ironic that General Schwarzkopf, who was at first reluctant to deploy the SAS as he felt that there was nothing that they could do that couldn't be done by air power and ground forces alone, later went on to write a letter of commendation to them. In the letter he openly and frankly stated how important their role had been in bringing about victory over the Iraqis, in what was a complicated and difficult operation.

In 2003, the SAS found itself back in Iraq fighting a war that for them mirrored the last one in many ways, yet differed in others. Essentially, their role was to prevent Iraqi surface-to-surface missile attacks, to engage the enemy on all fronts, to carry out covert reconnaissance, to cut Iraqi lines of communication and to designate targets for coalition aircraft, be it fielded forces or urban COGs. The SAS was deployed throughout Iraq in many different ways with squadrons mainly concentrated in the south and western regions, while smaller elements of the Regiment such as the highly secretive Increment, operated in north-eastern Iraq. Their mission was to train and coordinate the Kurdish Peshmerga forces as part of a joint UK/US operation. As in 1991, the SAS was extremely successful in its efforts, both covert and overt, and will no doubt use its recent experience as a model for future operations.

UK - THE SBS

In 2003, the SBS deployed to Iraq as part of Operation Telic where they performed superbly. Missions carried out included covert reconnaissance on the Al-Faw peninsula prior to the allied invasion and target designation against both fielded and urban based forces. In this role they identified a building in the city of Basra that contained some 200 Ba'ath party members and duly targeted both the building and its occupants. Other missions included acting as a tactical barometer for military operations where timing was critical, as in the siege of Basra, where the SBS identified the optimum moment for a large-scale attack by British Armour.

AIR CAVALRY - 16 AIR ASSAULT BRIGADE.

In 2003, 16 AAB deployed to Iraq as part of a major operation to secure valuable oilfields in the south of Iraq as there were grave fears that Iraqi militants would blow them up as part of a strategy to hinder allied forces during their liberation operation.

The operation was a great success and led to calls for the Brigade to be used elsewhere in the south as their skills were in high demand. 16 AAB responded by deploying forces in Basra where they became involved in numerous fierce firefights with the Fedayeen and their supporters. Other operations included mounting Eagle patrols as a means of denying enemy movement and sweep and clear missions to hunt down ring leaders and supporters of Saddam's hated regime.

95

THE ROYAL MARINES

The Royal Marines are an integral part of the Royal Navy, and were formed in 1942 as a commando force. Their current ORBAT (Order of Battle) comprises some 500 officers and 5,500 men, all highly trained and well equipped for both the rigours of land and sea warfare. By UK standards they are only deemed an elite force, but by any other they are Special Forces. The United States in particular, holds them in great esteem as they have a very close working relationship with the US Marine Corps.

The Royal Marines are always ready and willing to deploy at a moment's notice as they are a spearhead unit. The bulk of their manpower is grouped into lightly armed battalion-sized units known as commandos, of which there are currently three, and together they form 3 Commando Brigade. The Brigade is a key component of the UK's Joint Rapid Deployment Force (JRDF), and played a major role in fighting the Al-Qaeda terrorist network in Afghanistan prior to participating in the second Gulf War.

Above: Commandos in a canoe during the Second World War.

A Royal Marine Commando in Afghanistan.

British Commandos rehearsing an amphibious assault in preparation for the D-Day landings.

ROYAL MARINES' WEAPONS

Weapons used by the Royal Marines include the SA-80A2 assault rifle, the SA-80A2 LSW (Light Support Weapon), the 5.56 Minimi SAW (Squad Assault Weapon), the 7.62 GPMG (General Purpose Machine Gun), the Colt M4 assault rifle, the M16A2 assault rifle, the M203 Grenade launcher and the HK-MP5 sub-machine gun.

The Royal Marines' Amphibious Force deployed on Operation Telic, comprised of some 4,000 personnel drawn from the following units.

40 Commando Royal Marines
42 Commando Royal Marines
45 Commando Royal Marines
29 Regiment, Royal Artillery (equipped with 105mm light guns)
539 Assault Squadron, RM
59 Commando Squadron, RE
Plus elements of the SBS (Special Boat Service)

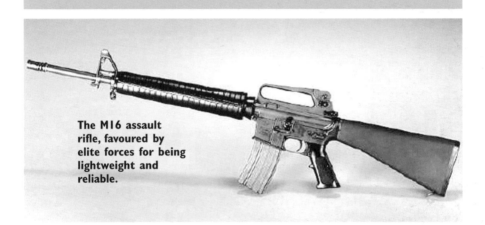

The M16 assault rifle, favoured by elite forces for being lightweight and reliable.

BRIGADE RECCE FORCE (BRF)

The Brigade Recce Force is the eyes and ears of the UK's elite amphibious force, the Royal Marines, and is tasked with covert intelligence gathering deep behind enemy lines (deep being described as anything beyond fifty kilometres or more).

The unit was born out of the highly regarded Royal Marines Mountain & Arctic Warfare Cadre and compares in many ways with the Parachute Regiment's Pathfinders - in effect they are an elite within an elite.

Although primarily tasked with covert reconnaissance and intelligence gathering, the unit also has a secondary role of providing an arctic and alpine warfare capability, both covert and overt, and works very closely with the

The BRF are the eyes and ears of the Royal Marines and the best of the best.

97

Royal Marines Commando Brigade Patrol Troops.

During Operation Telic, the BRF led the way for the Royal Marines as they assaulted the Al-Faw peninsula, operating in a manner very similar to that of the Royal Marines Special Forces, the SBS (Special Boat Service).

BRIGADE RECCE FORCE WEAPONS

Weapons used by the Brigade Recce Force include the SA-80A2 assault rifle, SA-80A2 LSW (Light Support Weapon), M16A2 assault rifle with M203 grenade launcher, Colt M4 assault rifle, H&K MP5 sub-machine gun, M249 Minimi SAW (Squad Assault Weapon) and, of course, the GPMG (General Purpose Machine Gun).

The Minimi SAW (Squad Assault Weapon), fitted with pre-packed, link ammunition.

THE CIA'S SPECIAL OPERATIONS GROUP (SOG)

The CIA's Special Operations Group (SOG) is the agency's secret army and was formed in the late 1990s to combat the rise in global terrorism. The CIA, of course, is no stranger to paramilitary operations having been involved in numerous covert activities over the years, some successful and some not so successful; the Bay of Pigs incident in Cuba being the most infamous.

Because of past failures and scandals, the CIA was forced to adopt a low profile for many years, but the events of 11 September 2001 brought it back into the covert paramilitary business with a new found purpose and a new determination - that being to protect America and its interests, both at home and overseas.

The architect of the modern SOG is the CIA's current director, George Tenet, who first began rebuilding the unit upon his appointment in 1999. Originally, the plan was to build up a new and enhanced operational capability before declaring the force ready and available, but the attacks of 9-11 threw that game plan out of the window..

Now with America facing its worst domestic crisis since Pearl Harbor, the decision was taken to deploy the SOG into Afghanistan as soon as possible; the rationale being that it gave America an unofficial covert presence on the ground prior to the official predicted military response.

In part this was an understandable decision as the CIA is America's eyes and ears and who in America is better trained or equipped than them to carry out such a task? The answer, of course is no one, as the SOG is renowned for its ability to infiltrate the indigenous population of a country both by fair and foul means.

George Tenet, director of CIA operations.

In essence SOG operators are not soldiers but spies who are trained to fight in an unconventional manner, very much in the vein of a guerrilla force, which makes them perfect for encouraging insurrection and revolt amongst a disaffected population. In the dim and distant past, traditional CIA officers tended to garner intelligence via embassy cocktail circuits or by bribing foreign officials, their cover generally being that of a US diplomat or a businessman. These days however, the methods are far more sophisticated in one way, yet more crude and brutal in others. They include the use of unmanned aircraft such as the Predator, a platform that is capable of photographing a footprint from some twelve miles away, while on the ground they have their operators who carry out missions either alone or in small teams, their role being to infiltrate enemy territory with extreme prejudice. Assassinations, targeting, coups, kidnappings and encouraging insurrection are all in a day's work, with action and varied work practically guaranteed as demonstrated during Operation Iraqi Freedom.

The SOG is the new hard edge of the CIA and is perfect for targeting unconventional forces such as Al-Qaeda and the Fedayeen Saddam, as they fight like terrorists and have no clearly defined territory or purpose, save for that of killing. In essence, the SOG takes the war to the level of the terrorist, employing combatants that are willing, adaptable and, at times, ruthless as fear is the key

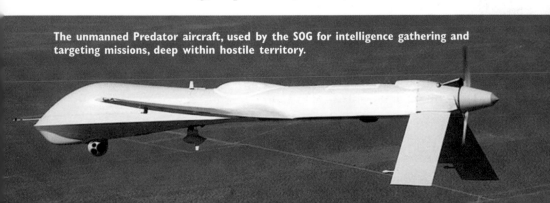

The unmanned Predator aircraft, used by the SOG for intelligence gathering and targeting missions, deep within hostile territory.

to the destruction and demise of a terrorist group.

The use of such operatives however, is not without its critics and indeed in America there is much concern as to the methods employed by the SOG and indeed the US Army's unconventional Gray Fox unit. The US military is also not too impressed with the idea of an unconventional guerrilla type force waging war by its side, especially as it virtually has carte blanche to do what it likes with little or no apparent accountability. The view of the US Special Forces is that they can perform any mission profile that the SOG is capable of and probably more efficiently. The SOG, however, takes the view that only it is capable of infiltrating enemy territory without arousing attention, especially in large towns and cities where it is imperative to have safe houses and network contacts. This argument indeed has much merit, as members of the SOG and Gray Fox spent months operating clandestinely within Baghdad without being compromised; many of these prior to Operation Iraqi Freedom.

SOG operative, Johnny (Mike) Spann who was tragically killed by Taliban fighters.

As a point of interest, the SOG had men operating on the ground in Afghanistan within fifteen days of 9-11, while US military forces took until 7 October before they commenced official retaliatory operations under the banner of Operation Enduring Freedom.

It was during this conflict that the SOG lost its first member, Johnny (Mike) Spann, thirty-two, who was killed near Mazar-e-sherif, during a revolt by Al-Qaeda/Taliban (AQT) prisoners shortly after he had interrogated them.

Although a setback for the group, it was not a show stopper and, if anything, it only served to galvanize their determination to see the job through. Shortly after the collapse of the Taliban regime, the SOG was in action again, only this time the venue was Yemen. Having received an intelligence tip-off that one of bin Laden's lieutenants, Mohammed Atef, was at large in the country

Below left: A Taliban soldier being interrogated in Mazar-e-sherif prison camp. Bottom right: Johnny Spann's body returns home with full military honours.

and indeed planning other attacks, the SOG went to work.

Using an ex-USAF Predator UAV, the SOG modified it to carry Hellfire missiles and, in an operation that was the first of its kind - not to mention highly controversial, they attacked the Al-Qaeda leader and his entourage, killing all in the process. Not content with their success, they set about devising further operations involving UAVs but these were put on hold pending the small matter of fighting in another war, only this time it was against an evil regime and not a terrorist group. The location this time was Iraq and, in anticipation of the forthcoming war, the SOG quietly sneaked into the Kurdish held enclaves in the northern part of the country and began recruiting a guerrilla

A US military adviser looks on the Taliban/Al-Qaeda uprising while holding a AK 47.

force. The Kurds already had the Peshmerga, a tough and resilient group who were greatly feared by the Iraqis and were perfect for the SOG's envisaged plans.

During Operation Iraqi Freedom, the SOG guided American forces through hostile areas, set up safe houses for downed pilots and Special Forces, mapped areas for potential targets and helped encourage insurrection amongst the Iraqi people, both with the Kurds in the north and the dissident Shi'ites in the south. Concerned at the rise in their popularity, the US Defense Secretary Donald Rumsfeld set about creating his own version of the CIA's SOG. Known as Gray Fox or the Army's Intelligence Support Activity (ISA), the unit is essentially a death squad and a re-creation of the Vietnam War Operation Phoenix assassination programme, only better trained and equipped. Essentially, Gray Fox is employed as the intelligence gathering arm of Task Force 20: its mission to track down Saddam Hussein and any of his remaining cronies.

Taliban fighters pose for the camera while on patrol.

At present within the Washington corridors of power, there is something of a power struggle taking place between George Tenet of the CIA and Donald Rumsfeld of the Department of Defense. This stems from the fact that Rumsfeld is deeply worried about the SOG's rapid rise in power and mission capability and is concerned that if it is not checked politically it may start wars that his military forces may have to finish, hence the formation of Gray Fox. As he controls it, he deploys it and he decides its missions. The SOG however is proving highly successful in its latest guise, so much so that it was recently put forward to resolve the North Korean problem once and for all.

There is no doubting its recent achievements in Afghanistan, Yemen and Iraq, particularly those with the Northern Alliance in Afghanistan, although the two cases containing $3,000,000 that the SOG gave them may have helped in motivating them. Anyone interested in joining this group will be handled in the following way.

Prospective recruits will be sent to the 'Farm' or, to give it its official designation, the agency's Camp Peary training centre, located on 9,000 acres of heavily wooded land near Williamsburg, Virginia. The camp is surrounded by barbed-wire topped fences and motion detectors.

During the year long stint at Camp Peary recruits will be taught such skills of the trade as infiltrating hostile countries, communicating in codes, retrieving messages from dead drops and recruiting foreign agents to spy for the US. In addition to stealing secrets for Uncle Sam, they will be taught how to blow up bridges, bring down aircraft and, of course, the art of assassination. However, most of their time will probably be spent using the laptop computers with which they are supplied for sending back reports from afar. Other skills taught include sharp shooting with various kinds of weapons, both US and foreign, setting up landing zones in remote areas of the world, as the agency does make extensive use of all types of aircraft and helicopters as demonstrated by 'Air America' in Vietnam. For some there will be training at Fort Bragg, the home of Delta Force, and for others there will be field deployments with various members of the Special Forces to whom they have been temporarily assigned.

Since 9-11 the focus of the SOG is counter-terrorism and over recent years the group has seen more than its fair share of the action, having carried out some of the CIA's most dangerous assignments. In the main foyer of the agency's Langley, Virginia, headquarters there is a wall that commemorates all of those that have fallen in the service of the CIA since it was founded in 1947. Of interest is the fact that almost half the seventy-nine stars chiselled into the wall belong to paramilitary officers, the newest being that of Johnny (Mike) Spann. At the time of writing this book, no details have been released of SOG casualties during Operation Iraqi Freedom but, no doubt, in the future we shall hear of their exploits.

Whatever you may think of the SOG and its unconventional methods and practices, it is a vital tool in America's arsenal in the war against terrorism and has a tenacious determination to get the job done. Its operators are also some of the most courageous and selfless men and women in the service of the United States today, operating in an environment of constant danger and uncertainty, with little chance of survival if compromised, and little chance of thanks if successful. For them it's not a job, it's an adventure.

USA - DELTA FORCE WEAPONS

Weapons and equipment used by Delta Force include the Colt M4 assault rifle, M16A2 assault rifle, Mini 14 assault rifle, Steyr AUG assault rifle, HK-G3 assault rifle, SOPMOD (Special Operations Peculiar Modification) M4A1 assault rifle, CAR 15 assault rifle, Stoner SR-25 self loading rifle and Colt Model 733 assault rifle. Walther MP-K SMG, HK-MP5SD SMG, MAC 10 SMG, and UZI SMG.

M249 SAW light machine gun, HK-13E light machine gun, M60 medium machine gun, M240B medium machine gun and Browning M2 .50 heavy machine gun.

Remington 870 combat shotgun and Mossberg Cruiser 500 combat shotgun, HK-PSG-sniper rifle, M40A1 sniper rifle, M24 sniper rifle and Barret M82A1 .50 heavy sniper rifle.

Support weapons include the M203 40mm Grenade launcher, M79 'Blooper' 40mm Grenade launcher, 81mm Mortar, Carl Gustav 84mm recoilless rifle, 66mm LAW and Mk 19 40mm automatic grenade launcher, Stinger MANPAD and the M136 AT-4 anti-tank rocket.

Beretta 92F handgun and SIG-Sauer P-228 handgun. Specialist Weapon Sights include Aimpoint Comp M close quarter battle sight, M68 Aimpoint, M28 Aimpoint sight, AN /PEQ2 Infrared Target Pointer/Illuminator/ Aiming laser (IPITAL) dual beam aiming device.

Uniforms worn by Delta Force include standard US Army combat fatigues, Lizard suits, Ghillie sniper suits and black Nomex overalls which are worn during counter-terrorist operations. Delta Operators also make extensive use of body armour and night vision devices such as the AN /PVS-7 night vision goggles and, for additional protection, they wear Bolle T800 ballistic goggles while operating in open areas. During counter-terrorist operations, Delta operators wear British Avon S10 respirators, body armour, anti-laser goggles and Nomex clothing.

Delta also operates an extensive fleet of vehicles that includes the Land-Rover Defender 110 SOV (Special Operations Vehicle), Humvee, Quad ATV (All Terrain Vehicle), Harley-Davidson Track Bike and LSV (Light Strike Vehicle). Weapons mounted on vehicles include Mk 19 40mm automatic grenade launchers, M60 medium machine guns, M240B medium machine gun, General Electric 7.62 mini gun, 20mm cannon and Browning M2 .50 Heavy machine gun.

Other specialist Delta equipment includes Zodiac boats, submersibles, high speed patrol boats and rigid raiders. Delta also uses heavily modified parachutes for its HALO and HAHO parachute operations.

The most common means of transport for Delta Force is the helicopter. Types used include the MH-47 D/E Chinook, MH-60 K/L Blackhawk and MH-6 Little Bird, which are operated by the US Army's 160th Special Operations Aviation Regiments. For long range missions, Delta uses the MH-53J which is operated by the USAF's Special Operations Group (SOG).

PVS-7 night vision goggles.

Sig Sauer P-228.

Beretta 92F.

Delta is extremely well funded and can buy almost any weapon or piece of equipment it wants without going through laborious purchasing procedures and is probably the best equipped Special Forces unit in the world

DELTA FORCE OPERATIONAL HISTORY

1979: Worked alongside the FBI during the Pan American Games in Puerto Rico as part of an anti-terrorist team that was set up in anticipation of a possible terrorist attack.

1980: Deployed to Iran to rescue American hostages who were being held by Iranian fundamentalists in Tehran. However, shortly after a decision was taken to abort the mission a helicopter collided with a transport aircraft on the ground which left eight American servicemen dead.

1983: Participated in Operation Urgent Fury in Grenada and carried out a helicopter assault on Richmond Hill Prison where a number of local government officials were being held hostage. They also assisted other units in seizing a key airfield during the initial assault phase.

1984: Sent to the Middle East after two Americans were killed during the hijacking of a Kuwait Airways airliner.

1985: Deployed to Cyprus in response to another hijacking, only this time it was an American aircraft owned by the airline TWA.

1987: Deployed to Greece following a report that Vietnamese agents were going to kill US Army Colonel James Rowe.

1989: Participated in Operation Just Cause in Panama, where they successfully rescued an American citizen who was being held hostage in Panama City. They also helped in the capture of General Manuel Noriega.

1991: Took part in Operation Desert Storm during the Gulf War where they provided protection for senior US officers and helped locate and destroy Iraq's mobile SCUD launchers.

Iranians inspect the wreckage of a US Navy helicopter in which Delta Force operatives were killed, attempting to rescue US hostages held in Tehran, 1980.

1993: Deployed to Mogadishu, Somalia as part of Task Force Ranger where they mounted numerous operations against Somali warlords, one of which ended in a major battle that left eighteen Americans dead and seventy badly injured. The Somalis however lost over 500 men.

1995: Deployed to Bosnia as part of an international effort to find Serbian war criminals.

1997: Sent to Lima, Peru along with six members of the British SAS following the takeover of the Japanese Ambassador's residence.

1999: Deployed to Kosovo in support of US Forces operating against the Federal Republic of Yugoslavia.

2001: Following the events of 11 September and under the designation of Task Force 11, Delta was deployed to Afghanistan in search of AQT (Al-Qaeda/Taliban) forces, in particular their leader Osama bin Laden.

2003: Deployed to Iraq under the designation of Task Force 20, and worked alongside the highly secretive Gray Fox unit, its mission being to hunt down Saddam Hussein and any of his fellow Regime members that are still at large following Operation Iraqi Freedom.

GRAY FOX

Of all the units currently operating in Iraq at this time, there are none that have generated as much debate as the US Army's Gray Fox unit. This stems from the fact that Gray Fox is essentially a death squad, set up for the purpose of carrying out high-value player assassinations, very much in the same manner as those carried out under the Vietnam era Operation Phoenix assassination programme.

The unit was set up prior to Operation Iraqi Freedom by the US Defense Secretary Donald Rumsfeld. It is effectively run by the US Army's Intelligence Support Activity (ISA), and serves as an Intel capability for Task Force 20, and indeed Task Force 11 which is concerned with the ongoing war against terrorism.

Gray Fox is well armed and equipped for its operational role and has access to virtually every type of modern weapon available, including those of the former Iraqi Army. Although the unit is capable of operating anywhere within Iraq, it tends to focus its efforts around central and northern Iraq as these are proving to be fertile areas for insurrection and revolt. They tend to be the areas most susceptible to hostile action against coalition forces often encouraged and orchestrated by former members of Saddam's regime.

Gray Fox has generally been very successful in its operations against former regime members, including Saddam's sons Uday and Qusay, who were killed as a result of an intelligence tip-off.

THE GREEN BERETS

The main role of the Green Berets is, when directed, to deploy and conduct unconventional warfare, foreign internal defence, special reconnaissance and direct action missions in support of US national policy objectives within the designated areas of responsibility.

The Green Berets are organized in a formation known as the 12-man Operations Detachment 'A', usually known as an 'A' team. This unit is the key operating element of the force, and five of these 'A' teams make up a 'B' team, which comprises six officers (including the major commanding the unit) and eighteen men. There are twelve 'A' teams per company, five companies per battalion and three battalions per group. At present there are seven groups, three regular, two National Guard and two reserve.

All members of the Green Berets are volunteers, who must be parachute qualified, either before joining or after. Once accepted for training, candidates participate in a rigorous training programme that lasts for sixty weeks. Those that qualify undergo a further period of training in advanced skills, including demolition, signals, engineering, languages, communications and intelligence gathering. All Green Berets must be specialists in at least two skills and can volunteer for advanced parachute courses, such as HALO and HAHO.

The famous motto of the Green Berets is 'De oppresso Liber' (meaning 'freedom from oppression').

During Operation Iraqi Freedom the Green Berets deployed to northern Iraq, their primary mission being to galvanize friendly, indigenous forces such as the Kurdish Peshmerga into a cohesive fighting unit. They were also tasked with providing a harassment capability against dug-in Iraqi forces, especially those located in and around the northern oil fields, providing a

Green Berets operating behind Iraqi enemy lines.

Green Berets undergoing training for urban warfare.　　**Sniper training in dense undergrowth.**

buffer force between the Iraqis and the Kurds, as there were well-founded fears and concerns as to the possibility of revenge attacks and even civil war once hostilities had ended and, finally, to provide a reconnaissance and intelligence gathering capability for coalition forces operating in the area, including those of the aircrews tasked with supporting the northern front, as they relied heavily on ground based Intel assets for mission tasking.

GREEN BERET WEAPONS

Weapons and equipment used by the Green Berets include the Colt M4 assault rifle, M16A2 assault rifle, Mini 14 assault rifle, SOPMOD (Special Operations Peculiar Modification) M4A1 assault rifle, CAR 15 assault rifle, Stoner SR-25 self loading rifle and Colt Model 733 assault rifle. Walther MP-K SMG, HK-MP5SD SMG, MAC 10 SMG, and UZI SMG. M249 SAW light machine gun, HK-13E light machine gun, M60 medium machine gun, M240B medium machine gun and Browning M2 .50 heavy machine gun.

Remington 870 combat shotgun and Mossberg Cruiser 500 combat shotgun, HK-PSG-sniper rifle, M40A1 sniper rifle, M24 sniper rifle and Barret M82A1 .50 heavy sniper rifle.

Support weapons include the M203 40mm Grenade launcher, 81mm Mortar, 66mm LAW, Mk 19 40mm automatic grenade launcher, Stinger MANPAD and the M136 AT-4 anti-tank rocket. Personal weapons include the Beretta 92F handgun and the SIG-Sauer P-228 handgun.

Specialist weapon sights include the Aimpoint Comp M close quarter battle sight, M68 Aimpoint, M28 Aimpoint sight and the AN /PEQ2 Infrared Target Pointer/Illuminator/Aiming laser (IPITAL) dual beam aiming device.

Uniforms worn by the Green Berets include standard US Army combat fatigues, Lizard suits and jungle tiger suits. The Green Berets also make extensive use of body armour and night vision devices such as the AN /PVS-7 night vision goggle, and while operating in urban, dusty or sandy conditions, they wear Bolle T800 ballistic goggles.

They operate an extensive fleet of vehicles both commercial and military, such as the Land-Rover Defender 110 SOV (Special Operations Vehicle), Humvee, Quad ATV (All Terrain Vehicle), and the Harley-Davidson Track Bike. Vehicle mounted weapons include Mk 19 40mm automatic grenade launchers, M60 medium machine guns, M240B medium machine guns, General Electric 7.62 mini guns, 20mm cannons and Browning M2 .50 heavy machine guns.

Other specialist Green Beret equipment includes Zodiac boats, high speed patrol boats, rigid raiders and heavily modified parachutes for HALO and HAHO type operations. The most common means of transport for the Green Berets is the helicopter. Types used include the MH-47 D/E Chinook, MH-60 K/L Blackhawk, MH-6 Little Bird, which are operated by the US Army's 160th Special Operations Aviation Regiment, while for long range missions, the Green Berets use the MH-53J which is operated by the USAF's Special Operations Group (SOG).

M16 203 with 40mm grenade launcher.

THE 75TH RANGER REGIMENT CONSISTS OF THREE BATTALIONS AND IS THE UNITED STATES' KEY SPEARHEAD UNIT.

THE RANGER CREED

Recognizing that I volunteered as a Ranger, fully knowing the hazards of my chosen profession, I will always endeavour to uphold the prestige, honour and high esprit de corps of my Ranger Regiment.

Acknowledging the fact that a Ranger is a more elite soldier who arrives at the cutting edge of battle by land, sea or air, I accept the fact that as a Ranger my country expects me to move further, faster and fight harder than any other soldier.

Never shall I fail my comrades. I will always keep myself mentally alert, physically strong and morally straight and I will always shoulder more than my share of the task, whatever it may be; one hundred per cent and then some.

Gallantly will I show the world that I am a specially selected and well trained soldier. My courtesy to superior officers, neatness of dress and care of equipment shall set the example for others to follow.

Energetically will I meet the enemies of my country. I shall defeat them on the field of battle for I am better trained and will fight with all my might. Surrender is not a Ranger word. I will never leave a fallen comrade to fall into the hands of the enemy and, under no circumstances, will I ever embarrass my country.

Readily will I display the internal fortitude required to fight on to the Ranger objective and complete the mission, though I be the lone survivor.

'Rangers lead the way.'

MAJOR ROBERT ROGERS

Although Major Robert Rogers wrote these standing orders during the seventeenth century, many of his tactics, techniques and procedures are still relevant today, with many of them practised as a matter of routine by those who serve in the modern day Special Forces. Major Robert Rogers was indeed a remarkable man to have had such foresight and vision all those years ago.

NINETEEN STANDING ORDERS

1. Don't forget anything.

2. Have your musket clean as a whistle, hatchet scoured, sixty rounds powder and ball, and be ready to march at a minute's warning.

3. When you're on the march, act the way you would if you was sneaking up on a deer. See the enemy first.

4. Tell the truth about what you see and what you do. There is an army depending on us for correct information. You can lie all you please when you tell other folks about the Rangers but don't ever lie to a Ranger or officer.

5. Don't ever take a chance you don't have to.

6. When we're on the march we march single file, far enough apart so no one shot can go through two men.

7. If we strike swamps, or soft ground, we spread out abreast, so it's hard to track us.

8. When we march, we keep moving till dark, so as to give the enemy the least possible chance at us.

Major Robert Rogers. His standing orders are still used by Special Forces to this day.

9. When we camp, half the party stays awake while the other half sleeps.

10. If we take prisoners, we keep 'em separate till we have had time to examine them, so they can't cook up a story between 'em.

11. Don't ever march home the same way. Take a different route so you won't be ambushed.

12. No matter whether we travel in big parties or little ones, each party has to keep a scout twenty yards ahead.

13. Every night you'll be told where to meet if surrounded by a superior force.

14. Don't sit down to eat without posting sentries.

15. Don't sleep beyond dawn. Dawn's when the French and Indians attack.

16. Don't cross a river at a regular ford.

17. If somebody's trailing you, make a circle, come back onto your own tracks, and ambush the folks that aim to ambush you.

18. Don't stand up when the enemy's coming against you. Kneel down, lie down, hide behind a tree.

19. Let the enemy come till he's almost close enough to touch. Then let him have it and jump out and finish him up with your hatchet.

US NAVY SEALS

The US Navy's SEAL (Sea-Air-Land) teams are the youngest of the United States Special Forces and together with their SEAL Delivery Vehicle Teams (SDV) and the Special Boat Squadrons (SBS) form the three branches of the US Navy's Special Warfare Command (NAVSPECWARCOM).

The SEALs specialize primarily in unconventional maritime warfare operations that include those of lakes, rivers, swamps and, of course, the sea. In some tactical situations such as those of Operation Iraqi Freedom, SEALs operated inshore in the same manner as conventional light infantry, but generally they tend to limit themselves to incursions that are no more than thirty-two kilometres (twenty miles) inland.

As with their other Special Forces colleagues, their roles and capabilities sometimes cross over with those of other units. For example, SEALs can perform light strike missions such as those undertaken by the US Rangers, while they in turn often use inshore craft for operations that are basically the same as those performed by the SEALs.

The difference, however, is in scale. According to a SEAL team commander:

'We in the SEALs are the United States military's small-unit maritime special operations force. We don't belong in anything that involves multi-pla-

Left: A US SEAL team operator scans for trouble.

A SEAL team carries out a search and sweep mission onboard a US Navy carrier. A prudent exercise that was carried out in light of the USS *Cole* attack.

The many combat roles of a US Navy SEAL. SEALs specialize in unconventional warfare both on land and sea and are masters of covert insertion techniques.

A SEAL on a reconnaissance mission.

toon operations - we've never been successful at it... We keep our units small and separate from large force operations. We have a niche here to be very good in units often less than eight men. That makes us harder to detect, easier to command and control, and better at the small unique operations we train for...'

A further difference is the environment. We keep one foot in the water. That means if we must do inland operations it is because they are attached to maritime reason. Keeping one foot in the water means that we don't get into areas that properly belong to other operators.'

Since their formation on 1 January 1962, the SEALs have seen action in Vietnam, Grenada, Panama, Columbia, Afghanistan and, of course, Iraq.

SEAL MISSION PROFILES

The US Navy SEALs operate according to five basic mission profiles; they are:

DIRECT ACTION: essentially combat operations, such as raiding, sabotage, hostage rescue and the capture of targets afloat or inshore.

SPECIAL RECONNAISSANCE: a SEAL speciality, the reconnaissance and surveillance of hostile territory, particularly beachheads. SEAL teams make beach surveys and like their predecessors (the UDTs), mark landing approaches and demolish obstacles and fortifications in preparation for an amphibious landing.

FOREIGN INTERNAL DEFENCE: the training of the military and security forces of friendly nations, usually in a non-combat environment.

UNCONVENTIONAL WARFARE: this is very much one of the reasons for John F. Kennedy's support for Special Forces. If required, the SEALs train, equip and lead guerrilla forces behind enemy lines.

COUNTER-TERRORIST OPERATIONS: the SEALs, particularly DEVGRU, conduct anti-terrorist operations, both reactive and preventative.

There are some 4,000 personnel in the US Navy Special Operations Forces, of which approximately 2,000 are SEALs. In theory, a full SEAL Team is made up of ten platoons of SEALs. However in practice, it is roughly thirty officers and 200 enlisted men strong. Within the ORBAT, there is a small support staff of non-SEALs - about twenty naval personnel. There is a command element, including the CO, executive officer and an operations officer - all of whom are fully qualified SEALs..Each platoon is sixteen men strong (two officers and fourteen men). The platoon divides into two squads (each with one officer and seven men), the squad being the preferred size for operations, while a squad sub-divides into two 4-man fire teams, each fire team comprising two swim pairs.

SBS AND SDV TEAMS

The Special Boat Squadrons (SBS) are known as the 'Brown Water Navy' and are the key to the whole US naval Special Forces set-up. They operate a variety of special operations craft, from fifty-two metres (170 feet) patrol boat coastal (PBC) vessels to rigid inflatable boats such as the five metres (fifteen feet) combat rubber raiding craft (CRRC), which are capable of reaching twenty knots.

The SBS essentially has three roles:

COASTAL PATROL AND INTERDICTION - this requires a reasonably large boat, so the mainstay of such missions is the PBC, which is large enough to carry both a significant weapons package and a sizeable SEAL and Naval Special Warfare force. Due to its size it can operate for extended periods of time without support, making it perfect for long range mission profiles.

FOR CLOSE INSHORE OPERATIONS - there is the twenty metres (sixty-five feet) MK III Swift Patrol Boat, a legacy of the 1960s and currently the subject of a replacement programme- its successor being the MK IV Patrol Boat. Some of these boats saw action in Iraq during Operation Iraqi Freedom, notably around the Al-Faw peninsula where they supported British, Australian and US forces as they fought their way from the deep water port of Umm Qasr up to the city of Basra. These boats were also used for protecting warships deployed offshore, as there were genuine fears of possible suicide attacks involving small speed boats and jet skis.

DURING CLANDESTINE OPERATIONS - the SEALs use rigid inflatable boats (RIBs) as they are small and stealthy and capable of high speeds in excess of twenty-five knots.

As with Vietnam, where the SEALs used riverine craft to great effect, the Iraq conflict also saw their deployment once again, mainly in and around the deep water port of Umm Qasr and its local waterways where they provided close protection for the Royal Marines, as they only had the use of landing craft, hovercraft and rigid raiders.

The standard vessels used by the SBS for this role are the Patrol Boat River (PBR), a ten metres (thirty-two feet) craft that is both well armed and equipped and is air-portable by C-5 Galaxy, while the smallest craft in the riverine inventory is the eight metres (twenty-five feet) Patrol Boat Light (PBL) which is air portable by helicopters such as the Chinook and the MH-53.

For covert sub-surface insertions, there is the SDV (Swimmer Delivery Vehicle) - in essence a mini-submarine that is capable of inserting small 6-man SEAL teams in all weathers, and usually reserved for highly classified missions.

At the height of Operation Iraqi Freedom, SEAL Teams were involved both inshore and offshore, while post war they have been heavily involved in land based operations - primarily supporting Task Force 20. Operations of note include the storming of two oil rigs located offshore from the Al-Faw peninsula, as the Iraqis had no time to blow them up on account of the SEALs swift actions. Inshore, there was excellent work done by SEAL teams riding shot-gun for the British Royal Marines, as they were equipped with both heavily armed riverine craft and hand-held reconnaissance UAVs (Unmanned Air Vehicles) that were perfect for scouting the marshy areas that surrounded Umm Qasr and its many tributaries.

However, the biggest and most important operation for the SEALs came after the end of Operation Iraqi Freedom, when they embarked on the massive US led manhunt for Saddam Hussein and his remaining henchmen, the mission being undertaken on behalf of Task Force 20 as the SEALs formed part of their ORBAT (Order of Battle).

SEAL TEAM WEAPONS

The SEALs have access to a wide variety of weaponry and choice is usually down to personal preference or mission profile. Weapons used include the CAR-15 assault rifle and the M16A2 assault rifle, both of which can mount the M203 40mm grenade launcher, and for extra stopping power the old but reliable 7.62mm M14 is still used. Close range weapons include the entire HK-MP5 family, as well as a customer specific model, the MP5K-PDW, which was designed specifically for NAVWARCOM use. For ship-boarding, urban and jungle work, the SEALs use 12-gauge shotguns such as the Remington Model 870 and the Franchi Spas, while for Squad fire support they generally operate the 5.56mm SAW and the 7.62mm M-60 machine gun.

Other weapons frequently seen on their vehicles and boats include the M2HB .50 calibre HMG, the MK-19 40mm grenade launcher and, of course, the good old M-60 machine gun.

Personal sidearms include the 9mm SIG Sauer P226, the .45 mm M1911A1, the .357 Smith and Wesson revolver, the 9mm HK P9S and the .45 HK Mk23 Mod O Special Operations Forces Offensive Handgun.

Vehicles used include the Humvee and the LSV (Light Strike Vehicle).

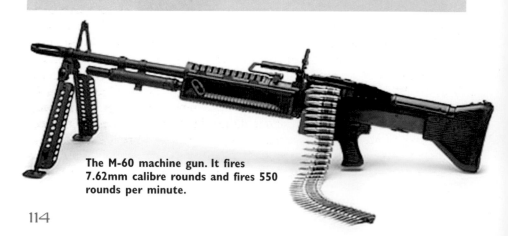

The M-60 machine gun. It fires 7.62mm calibre rounds and fires 550 rounds per minute.

TASK FORCE 11 OPERATIONAL HISTORY

2002: Deployed to the Philippines, Pakistan, Yemen, Saudi Arabia and Afghanistan as part of Operation Enduring Freedom.

2003: Deployed to Iraq as part of Operation Iraqi Freedom and Enduring Freedom following Saddam Hussein's failure to comply with UN resolution 1441. Also during this period, elements of Task Force 11 were deployed to South Korea following a rise in tensions between the United States and North Korea.

TASK FORCE 20

Task Force 20 was formed as a mission specific unit tasked with operating covertly against Iraqi forces, both conventional and unconventional, such as the Fedayeen Saddam during Operation Iraqi Freedom but now has the role of supporting conventional forces in post war Iraq, its mission being: to find and destroy Saddam Hussein's weapons of mass destruction and to find, kill or capture any remaining senior members of his Ba'ath Party regime still at large.

The name Task Force 20 reflects the date on which official hostilities commenced with Iraq under the banner of Operation Iraqi Freedom, that being 20 March 2003. The impetus for setting up such a force stems from the success of Task Force 11, a unit that was set up after 9-11 to prosecute an ongoing war against terrorism under the umbrella of Operation Enduring Freedom. Indeed, some elements of this force were involved in actual combat operations in Iraq as there was already a proven link between Iraq and terrorism.

Task Force 20 is primarily composed of operators drawn from Delta Force who act both as the cutting edge and the core of the unit, while elements of the highly secretive Gray Fox unit provide its intelligence capability. Other units available to assist Task Force 20 in the execution of its duties include the US Navy's SEAL (Sea, Air, Land) teams, the USAF's SOG (Special Operations Group) and the US Army's 160th SOAR (Special Operations Aviation Regiment).

Since being deployed in Iraq, Task Force 20 has gained a reputation for being hard hitting, not to mention controversial. This stems from several operations mounted in Baghdad, where the unit has appeared to have shot first and asked questions afterwards. One such incident occurred on Sunday, 27 July 2003, when a car full of westerners in civilian garb driving an expensive customized 4x4 vehicle pulled up outside the Al Sa'ah restaurant in the wealthy Mansur district of Baghdad, and began observing the locals coming and going from the vicinity of Prince Rabiah Muhamed al-Habib's house some two blocks away. After a period of time, the men got out of the vehicle and slowly moved towards the house. As they did so, a small convoy of six US Army Humvees began sealing off the nearby roads, effectively acting as both a cut-off group and a perimeter security force. On a pre-arranged signal, there was a loud explosion from the Prince's house, followed by a flurry of activity from the nearby streets as men wearing gas masks, body armour and black T-shirts covered in brightly coloured identification vests stormed the house: their mission was to arrest Saddam's son, Ali.

As the operation progressed, crowds began to gather out of idle curiosity - a common trait in this region - especially during a military operation. The first casualties of this operation were the unlucky occupants of a Chevrolet Malibu that failed to stop for a perimeter security team that was located near to a make-shift Humvee road block. This was quickly followed by another incident, in which a Toyota Corolla driven by a disabled man and carrying both his wife and teenage son, was engaged by US forces after it had taken a wrong turning near another road block, resulting in the driver being killed and the others wounded.

The carnage however, was not yet over as another innocent victim was claimed on the nearby highway, his crime being that he slowed down to observe what was going on. His bullet riddled Mitsubishi Pajero bore testament to the price of his curiosity. According to locals who witnessed the event, the Americans were firing indiscriminately and wildly at anything that moved, a fact seemingly proven by the casualties themselves, as none was found with any weapons. In all, five innocent Iraqis lost their lives for nothing, as Saddam's son was not in the target house nor indeed had he been there for several months prior to this tragic event.

Fearing a back-lash from the Iraqi people, the US Military apologized for what had taken place and promised to be more careful next time. It was during this apology that details were released for the first time as to the purpose of Task Force 20 and indeed its mission in Iraq. It confirmed that since the end of Operation Iraqi Freedom, Task Force 20 had been involved in numerous operations to flush out Saddam and his followers, with many of them taking place in the myriad of underground bunkers and tunnels that criss-crossed Baghdad.

Although the US Military is generally tight-lipped about its Special Forces activities in Iraq, it has been remarkably candid when it comes to Task Force 20. It acknowledged that during the war the unit had fought in the western desert against conventional Iraqi forces but had failed to find any weapons of mass destruction during these operations. Ironically its most notable success came after the end of Operation Iraqi Freedom when it was involved in the 22 July raid in Mosul, that resulted in the deaths of Saddam's evil sons Uday and Qusay.

Elsewhere in Iraq, while operating out of Baghdad International Airport, Task Force 20 mounted a series of intensive operations in Saddam's hometown of Tikrit but failed to find him.

Task Force 20 is believed to comprise 750 operational personnel drawn from Special Operations Command, but there are no official figures to verify this. One thing for sure, Task Force 20 has its work cut out in Iraq, as keeping the peace is proving to be far more demanding than winning the war ever was.

TASK FORCE 20 WEAPONS AND EQUIPMENT

Weapons and equipment used by Task Force 20 include the Colt M4 assault rifle, M16A2 assault rifle, Mini 14 assault rifle, SOPMOD (Special Operations Peculiar Modification) M4A1 assault rifle, CAR 15 assault rifle, Stoner SR-25 self loading rifle and Colt Model 733 assault rifle.

Walther MP-K SMG, HK-MP5SD SMG and MAC 10 SMG M249 SAW light machine gun, HK-13E light machine gun, M60 medium machine gun, M240B medium machine gun and Browning M2 .50 heavy machine gun.

Remington 870 combat shotgun and Mossberg Cruiser 500 combat shotgun, HK-PSG-sniper rifle, M40A1 sniper rifle, M24 sniper rifle and Barret M82A1 .50 heavy sniper rifle.

Support weapons include the M203 40mm grenade launcher, 81mm Mortar, 66mm LAW and Mk 19 40mm automatic grenade launcher and the Stinger MANPAD. Personal weapons include the Beretta 92F handgun and the SIG-Sauer P-228 handgun. Specialist weapon sights include Aimpoint Comp M close quarter battle sight, M68 Aimpoint, M28 Aimpoint sight, AN /PEQ2 Infrared Target Pointer/Illuminator/Aiming laser (IPITAL) dual beam aiming device.

Uniforms when worn by Task Force 20 include standard US Army combat fatigues, Lizard suits, Urban Combat fatigues, Ghillie sniper suits and black Nomex overalls which are worn during hostage rescue type operations. Most operators however, choose to wear civilian clothing when operating covertly in Iraq as it makes it easier for them to blend in.

Task Force 20 operators also make extensive use of body armour and night vision devices such as the AN /PVS-7 night vision goggle. While operating in dusty and sandy conditions they wear personal eye protection such as the Bolle T800 ballistic goggle, and while participating in counter-terrorist type operations they wear British Avon S10 respirators, close protection Kevlar body armour, anti-laser goggles and Nomex clothing.

Task Force 20 also operates an extensive fleet of vehicles that include the Land-Rover Defender 110 SOV (Special Operations Vehicle), Humvee, Quad ATV (All Terrain Vehicle), Harley-Davidson Track Bike and LSV (Light Strike Vehicle). Weapons mounted on vehicles include Mk 19 40mm automatic grenade launchers, M60 medium machine guns, M240B medium machine guns, General Electric 7.62 mini guns, 20mm cannons and Browning M2 .50 heavy machine guns. Other specialist equipment includes Zodiac boats, submersibles, high speed patrol boats and rigid raiders. Task Force 20 also uses heavily modified parachutes for its HALO and HAHO parachute operations.

Although the most common means of transport for Task Force 20 is the helicopter, they will use literally anything available, including horses..In Iraq however, they tend to use commercial 4 x4 vehicles as they generate far less attention. Helicopter types used include the MH-47 D/E Chinook, MH-60 K/L Blackhawk and MH-6 Little Bird, which are operated by the US Army's 160th Special Operations Aviation Regiment. For long range missions, Task Force 20 uses the MH-53J, which is operated by the USAF's Special Operations Group (SOG).

Barret M82A1 .50
heavy sniper rifle.

UNITED STATES MARINE CORPS (USMC)

USMC units deployed during Operation Iraqi Freedom included:

Marine Expeditionary Force
1st Marine Division
1st Marine Regiment
3rd Battalion, 1st Marines
1st Battalion, 4th Marines
1st, 3rd Battalions, Light Armoured Recon

5th Marine Regiment
1st Battalion, 5th Marines
2nd, 3rd Battalions, 5th Marines

7th Marine Regiment
1st, 3rd Battalions, 7th Marines
3rd Battalion, 4th Marines
3rd Battalion, 11th Marines
1st Tank Battalion

2nd Marine Expeditionary Brigade, 2nd Marine Division
1st, 3rd Battalions, 2nd Marines
2nd Battalion, 8th Marines
1st Battalion, 10th Marines
2nd Amphibious Assault Battalion
2nd Recon Battalion
2nd Light Armoured Recon Battalion
2nd, 8th Tank Battalions

15th Marine Expeditionary Unit

24th Marine Expeditionary Unit

26th Marine Expeditionary Unit

CHAPTER FOUR

SPECIAL FORCES: THE FACE OF FUTURE WARFARE

*'They move around the battlefield unseen, unheard and unsung.
They take on seemingly impossible missions both alone and
with conventional forces.
No one knows when they leave or when they come back or
even how many started out.
They are the best that their countries have to offer.
They are Special Forces, and they are the best of the best.
They are the face of future warfare.'*

Following the events of 11 September 2001, the words 'special
forces' have dominated the world's headlines as they are seen
as the key tool in future warfare against both terrorists and
conventional forces alike. Their ability to deploy unseen and unheard
gives their governments a powerful weapon that is both efficient and
effective as nobody knows when or where they will strike.

The idea of Special Forces is not new. The Ancient Greeks used the Trojan horse ploy to enter the city of Troy thus gaining the element of surprise.

Special Forces are used for both conventional and unconventional warfare and often act as spearhead units in advance of regular conventional forces. They are well trained and equipped for modern warfare and represent the best of their country's armed forces. They are highly motivated individuals that can make the difference between victory and defeat and in today's uncertain world that is no mean feat.

Since Operation Enduring Freedom first began in 2001, Special Forces have been portrayed as almost superhuman and indestructible. The massive media coverage that surrounded 9-11 gave the impression to the public that Special Forces were something new that had been created following the terrorist attack on the United States.

Of course the idea of Special Forces is nothing new, as there have been numerous examples throughout history of men performing unconventional operations that have either ended or shortened a conflict. Examples include the ploy of the Trojan Horse, used by the Greeks to insert soldiers into Troy, the city they were besieging and the Englishman Robert Rogers, who formed the Rangers, an elite group of men who raged an unconventional war with great success against the French and their allies, the North American Indians. In fact, some of his famous military standing orders and tactics are still valid to this day and are regularly taught and practised by today's Rangers, the 75th Ranger Regiment.

Special Forces are now a critical component of any modern army and they are playing an ever increasing role in today's warfare. Operational roles include covert reconnaissance, both tactical and strategic, hit and run, rescue of downed aircrew, sabotage, attacks on high value targets,

SAS soldiers on a counter-terrorism training exercise.

US Special Forces undergoing combat search and rescue training in the United States. This level of training has proved valuable in the rescue of pilots on many occasions in places such as Somalia, Bosnia and more recently, Iraq.

counter-terrorism, VIP protection and abduction of high value personnel such as war criminals and high ranking officers.

In future conflicts the role of Special Forces is likely to be substantially increased, particularly in the roles of intelligence gathering and target designation as you simply cannot beat having eyes and ears on the ground. This has been proved time and time again during operations in Bosnia, Kosovo, Afghanistan and Iraq. In all of these conflicts, Special Forces carried out close target recces (CTRS) on both high value targets and enemy fielded forces, which greatly increased the operational effectiveness of both airborne and ground based assets.

This intelligence gathering also helped to minimize collateral damage and civilian casualties; a key issue of modern warfare.

SPECIAL FORCES

Ask anyone to describe their visual image of a Special Forces soldier and they will probably give you a description of someone who is likely to be a cross between Sly Stallone in Rambo and Arnold Schwarzenegger in Commando. The truth is that over the years the movie industry has been working in overdrive producing a plethora of action films that portray Special Forces as muscle-bound meatheads with little intelligence. They assume that every Special Forces soldier walks around every day of the week with coils of ammunition belts and dozens of grenades about him, ready to take on the world without a second thought.

The truth of the matter however, is that they are not like their screen image in terms of physical and mental stature and, far from being loud-mouthed and arrogant, they are generally very quiet and unassuming men. There is a common thread that links Special Forces worldwide, and that is the stringent entry criteria. They simply want the best of the best and can afford to be very selective about who they recruit as these men and, in some cases, women may one day be required to serve their country.

SBS boat troop operative conducting a beach head recce.

Over the years I have worked with operators from many countries around the world and I have always been impressed with the fact that regardless of whether they were British, American, Australian or German they were all decent and honourable men who were clearly highly trained and extremely professional in their work. Apart from looking fit and healthy there was nothing distinguishing about them that would lead you to believe that they were Special Forces personnel and indeed many of them could easily walk into a bar or shopping mall without anyone looking at them twice, which is the ultimate test for those who want to be grey men (a person who blends into their surroundings without attracting attention to themselves).

Many people often ask questions about Special Operations and Special Forces and what their role is in modern warfare as they simply have no understanding of their specific purpose. According to the United States Special Operations Posture Statement 2000, the general meaning of the term 'Special Operations' is as follows:

'These are actions which are conducted by specially organized, trained and equipped military or paramilitary forces in order to

Australian SAS troopers stop to observe a possible threat while on a routine patrol in Afghanistan.

US Navy SEALs secure the deck of a ship after a boarding mission.

A Polish GROM Special Forces soldier, provides cover with his M16 assault rifle.

achieve military, political, economic or psychological objectives by unconventional means in hostile, denied or politically sensitive areas. They may be conducted in peacetime, in periods of conflict or during all-out war, independently or in coordination with conventional forces. The military and political situation frequently dictates such special operations, and such operations usually differ from conventional operations in their degree of risk, the operational techniques involved, their modus operandi, independence from friendly support and dependence upon essential operational intelligence, and the knowledge of the indigenous assets available'

THE US SPECIAL FORCES' CREED

I am an American Special Forces' soldier. A professional! I will do all that my nation requires of me. I am a volunteer, knowing well the hazards of my profession. I serve with the memory of those who have gone before me: Roger's Rangers, Francis Marion, Mosby's Rangers, the first Special Service Forces and Ranger Battalions of World War ll, the Airborne Ranger Companies of Korea. I pledge to uphold the honor and integrity of all I am - in all I do.

I am a professional soldier. I will teach and fight wherever my nation requires. I will strive always, to excel in every art and artifice of war.

I know that I will be called upon to perform tasks in isolation, far from familiar faces and voices, with the help and guidance of my God.

I will keep my mind and body clean, alert and strong, for this is my debt to those who depend on me.

I will not fail those with whom I serve.

I will not bring shame upon myself or the faces.

I will maintain myself, my arms, and my equipment in an immaculate state as befits a Special Forces' soldier.

I will never surrender though I be the last. If I am taken, I pray that I may have the strength to spy upon my enemy.

My goal is to succeed in any mission - and live to succeed again.

I am a member of my nation's chosen soldiery. God grant that I may not be found wanting, that I will not fail this sacred trust.

'It is not the critic who counts, not the man who points out how the strong man stumbled, or where the doer of deeds could have done better. The credit belongs to the man who is actually in the arena; whose face is marred by the dust and sweat and blood; who strives valiantly; who errs and comes short again and again; who knows the great enthusiasms, the great devotions and spends himself in a worthy course; who at the best, knows in the end the triumph of high achievement, and who, at worst, if he fails, at least fails while daring greatly; so that his place shall never be those cold and timid souls who know neither victory or defeat.'

THEODORE ROOSEVELT (Paris, Sorbonne, 1910)

Modern warfare wears many faces, ranging from large conventional forces operating on peace keeping missions to stealth aircraft that can bomb targets deep behind enemy lines without being detected. However, the face of the Special Forces soldier is faceless as that is what keeps him alive. To be successful in today's unstable world, Special Forces operators have to be both mentally and physically fit as their world is a completely different one to that of a conventional soldier.

Throughout history small bands of warriors have waged war by using unusual and unconventional weapons, tactics and techniques to fight and defeat larger conventional forces. These groups were generally crude and often behaved in an unlawful way, which is not the way modern Special Forces operate.

'Perfect planning prevents poor performance'

Today Special Forces operators have high personal goals, with a second best performance being viewed as no performance at all. As the British SAS saying goes; *'perfect planning prevents poor performance'*, a statement that all professional soldiers respect and understand. The aim of the modern Special Forces operator is to be as close to the moral high ground as possible, and to become the most useful, resourceful and feared person on the battlefield.

In Afghanistan the role of the Special Forces soldier came under intense scrutiny as here was a war where aircraft, like the mighty B-52, were being used for close support bombing missions, an idea that would have been laughed at ten years ago, only made possible by small teams of highly trained and well equipped men that could operate right amongst the enemy forces, calling in air attacks with deadly accuracy and without being detected. In effect they were the precision weapons rather than the aircraft's bombs. Special Forces are also a great tool for governments that want an official footprint on the ground without

The mighty US B-52 heavy bomber. These were used for Special Forces close support bombing missions in Afghanistan and proved highly succesful in this role.

Above & left: US Navy SEALs on mountain patrol in Afghanistan.

risking conventional forces that could be highly vulnerable to attack. A good example of this tactic could be found in Oman during the 1970s when the British SAS waged a low intensity war against overwhelming guerrilla forces and defeated them. Yet hardly anyone in Britain knew about this war as only eighty British SAS soldiers were ever there at any given time.

Special Forces Operators are men and, in some cases, women who have been specially selected, specially trained and specially equipped to carry out special missions. Their use in a crisis is always considered first as they give politicians a chance to resolve a problem quietly and discreetly without drawing too much attention, compared with that generated when an aircraft carrier or a conventional battle group deploys. Also, in the event of things going wrong, the sensitive issue of casualties can be avoided as there is little chance of large scale losses in a small force, and no member of the media ever knows how many were deployed in the first place.

The role of Special Forces is growing all the time as they are seen as being capable of carrying out seemingly impossible missions such as during the first Gulf War in 1991, when British SAS and US Delta Force operators located and destroyed Iraqi mobile Scud missile launchers that had been causing severe

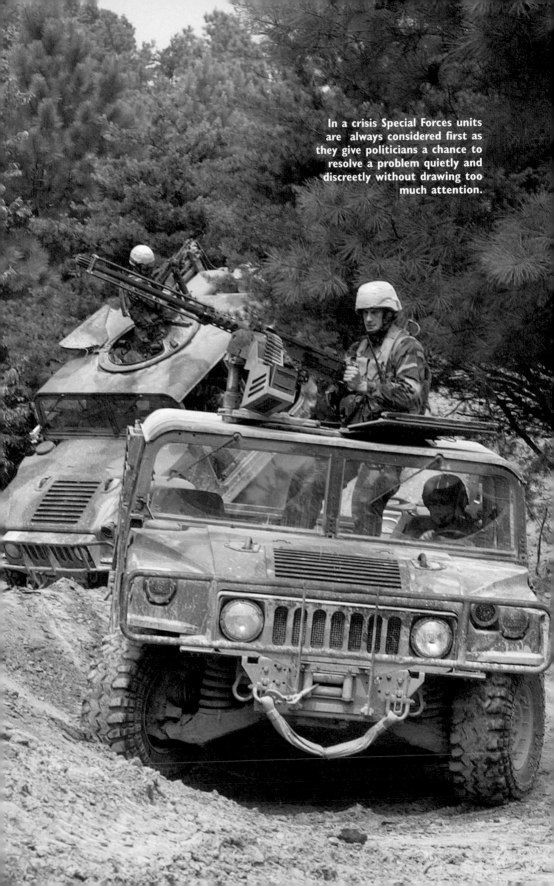

In a crisis Special Forces units are always considered first as they give politicians a chance to resolve a problem quietly and discreetly without drawing too much attention.

There is no simple way to mass produce Special Forces soldiers. This was proved in Vietnam when standards were dropped in an attempt to put more specialist soldiers in the field, the result being failure.

problems for the Allied Coalition Force. After the war ended there was a great impetus to create more of the same type of men that carried out these missions, but they cannot be mass produced as they are a very rare breed indeed.

One only has to look back at the American example in Vietnam to see what happens when standards are dropped to increase numbers of Special Forces personnel in the field. In their wisdom the Americans decided that more Special Forces equals quick victory but that was not to be the case. Indeed, with the standards lowered, the results fell too, the consequences of this being the premature withdrawal of many of them from Vietnam.

There is simply no way to mass produce Special Forces as their qualities are rarely found in Joe Average on the street. To be a member of any elite force is no easy matter as only the best candidates are selected. Training is usually divided into three phases.

Phase One: candidates are tested for physical fitness. This usually takes the form of punishing exercises designed to reveal psychological determination and character.

Phase Two: candidates are instructed in the key skills of the unit. This will involve weapons handling, tactical reconnaissance and covert operations.

Phase Three: candidates receive specialist instruction in subjects such as communication, sniping, demolition and CRW Operative.

Candidates can be rejected at any stage of the process and with courses lasting for almost a year this creates enormous mental pressure. The rejection rate for Special Forces is around eighty per cent, and the upshot of such rigorous selection is that only the most determined and intelligent make it. As the British SAS say, '*Death is God's way of telling you that you have failed selection*'.

Soldiers serving in Special Forces' units are generally multi-skilled as they need to be self sufficient. In addition to their combat skills, Special Forces soldiers also learn languages, engineering, defensive driving and combat medicine. In today's unpredictable and unstable world, units have to be able to deploy at very short notice. In some cases this can mean hours.

Special Forces can be sent literally anywhere in the world, so it is imperative for them to train in varied and diverse environments ranging from hot deserts to steamy, snake infested jungles. Deploying from one part of the world to another is no easy task as it often takes soldiers days and, in some cases, weeks to fully acclimatize. For instance a Special Forces soldier deploying from a lowland area in Europe to a mountainous region in Afghanistan will suffer a fifty per cent reduction in combat performance without adequate acclimatization time. Operating in a jungle environment is also very difficult on account of the constant dangers of heat exhaustion, poisonous snakes and infection and, if that is not enough, there is also the added worry of both booby traps and enemy ambushes with which to contend.

There is little point in a soldier fighting the jungle, as he simply will not win. The best solution is to make the jungle your friend and live with it and not against it, as your enemy will have the same problems as you. Special Forces are taught to both live and fight in the jungle until their reactions are second nature. Wars against indigenous forces can be fought and won in the jungle as the British SAS proved in both Malaya and Borneo. Jungle warfare will not die out for Special Forces in the future, that would be wishful thinking on behalf of the many guerrilla and terrorist groups that inhabit its hostile environment. Instead there is likely to be a new vigour to penetrate and dominate the world's jungles that offer sanctuary and succour to those who oppose our freedom and values.

> **'Death is God's way of telling you that you have failed selection'.**

Special Forces generally receive more funding and resources than conventional forces as their requirements are higher. The US 75th Ranger Regiment, which is only three battalions strong, receives more money than an entire division.

Since 9-11 there has been a dramatic increase in spending on Special Forces because of their great success in Afghanistan. This is in complete contrast to the Gulf War in 1991, where the appreciation of Special Forces and their capabilities prior to the conflict was somewhat limited, particularly within the US Military. This stemmed from the Vietnam War where the performance of Special Forces was called into question during the later stages of the conflict. Another major factor was the failure of Operation Eagle Claw in 1980, which was mounted following the seizure of American hostages in Iran. Although meticulously planned, the operation failed through a series of unforeseen events; the worst sand storm in living memory and a collision between a transport helicopter and a refuelling aircraft at a rendezvous point known as Desert One.

Prior to the launch of Operation Desert Storm, General Norman Schwarzkopf felt that air power alone would be enough to soften up the Iraqi forces before the ground invasion phase. His initial view was that Special Forces had no real part to play in this conflict as America and its allies in the coalition force had overwhelming air and ground forces at their disposal, which he felt were more than enough to win the war.

However, General Sir Peter de la Billière, the joint British Commander-in-Chief in the Gulf, was a veteran of the SAS and knew the value of such forces.

He persuaded General Schwarzkopf who, although sceptical at first, relented and gave permission for two SAS squadrons to be deployed on 20 January 1991. It was to be a highly significant decision as both the SAS and Delta Force played a key role in this conflict, especially in their operations against Saddam Hussein's Scud missiles.

After Desert Storm the entire attitude towards Special Forces changed both in the United States and elsewhere. They were now no longer deemed exotic, but essential.

Special Forces are generally far better armed and equipped than conventional forces as their operational requirements are much more demanding. In the case of both the British SAS and US Delta Force, a typical eight man patrol will carry more firepower than 100 conventionally armed soldiers. Their typical weapons include the M249 SAW (Squad Assault Weapon), Colt M4 assault rifle fitted with 40mm M203 grenade launcher, a machine gun such as the GPMG or M60, grenades, explosives, Claymore mines and usually a light armour weapon such as LAW 80 or AT-4. Personal kit usually consists of a side-arm, knife and a good old compass, while each team has at least one of the following items; a GPS, a secure radio with burst transmission capability, a Sat-phone and a TACBE.

All things considered, the United States has, without doubt, the best equipped Special Forces in the world.

The favoured weapons of US and UK Special Forces.

Colt Commando M4.

Colt Commando M4 fitted with M203.

M-60 E4 belt fed 7.62mm machine gun.

Browning High Power 9mm pistol

US issue fighting knife.

M249 SAW.

CHAPTER FIVE

COALITION, COMMAND & CONTROL STRUCTURES

US ARMY SPECIAL OPERATIONS COMMAND (USASOC)

Special Forces have been a part of American history since the seventeenth century when Major Robert Rogers decided that unconventional warfare had a place within the American armed forces of the day and set about forming America's first Special Forces unit, the Rangers.

Although individual officers and men have used unconventional tactics and strategies for hundreds of years, it only became apparent during the Second World War that there was a need for an official recognition of such forces. Although America had the Office of Strategic Services (OSS) which coordinated unconventional warfare during the war, its scope was limited and this eventually led to the formation of the 10th Special Forces Group in the early 1950s.

It was only when America became involved in Vietnam that things really started to change significantly for the better. This new attitude partly came about because of President Kennedy's interest in Special Operations Forces (SOF), in particular the Green Berets after he granted them permission to wear the distinctive beret for which they are now famous. After the Vietnam War ended, SOF capability declined within the US Army to such a degree that their entire future was in doubt. Things finally came to a head in 1980 following the failure of Operation Eagle Claw which led to the formation of the joint counter-terrorist task force and the Special Operations Advisory Panel. Following many years of soul searching and internal re-education of Special Forces and their future role within the US Armed Forces, the Department of Defense activated USSOCOM.

USSOCOM

USSOCOM consists of 46,000 Army, Navy and Air Force SOF personnel, both active and reserve. These forces are organized as follows:

US Army Special Forces: 75th Ranger Regiment, 160th Special Operations Aviation Regiment (SOAR) and psychological and civil affairs units.

US Navy: sea-air-land forces (SEALS), special boat units and SEAL delivery units.

US Air Force: special operations squadrons (fixed and rotary wing), a foreign internal defence squadron and a combat weather squadron.

A Joint Special Operations Command (JSOC).

USSOCOMs function is to provide highly trained rapidly deployable and regionally focused SOF personnel in support of global requirements from the

US Navy SEAL fast ropes onto the deck of a movingship during Operation Enduring Freedom.

national command authorities, the geographic commanders-in-chief (C.-in-C.) and the American ambassadors and their country teams. The geographic C.-in-C.'s area of responsibility (AOR) is divided into various commands. In 1999, SOF had units deployed in 152 countries and territories (not including classified missions and special access programmes). On any given day, some 5,000 SOF are deployed in sixty countries. The characteristics of SOF personnel are shaped by the requirements of their missions and include foreign language capabilities, regional orientation, specialized equipment, training and tactics, flexible force structure and an understanding of the political context of the mission.

US ARMY SPECIAL OPERATIONS COMMAND (USASOC)

Activated on 1 December 1989 and commanded by a lieutenant general, USASOC is the Army component of USSOCOM and controls:

Five active and two Army National Guard (ARNG) Special Forces groups totalling fifteen active and six ARNG battalions.

One active Ranger Regiment (75th) consisting of three battalions.

An active special operations aviation regiment (160th SOAR) with a detachment in Puerto Rico.

Four reserve civil affairs (CA) commands, seven reserve CA brigades, and one active and twenty-four reserve CA battalions.

One active and two reserve PSYOP groups totalling five active and eight reserve PSYOP battalions.

One active special operations support command composed of one special operations signal battalion (112th), one special operations support battalion (528th) and six special operations theatre support elements.

Two active and two reserve chemical reconnaissance detachments (CRD).

The John F. Kennedy Special Warfare Center and School.

SOAR - 'NIGHT STALKERS'

Following the failure of Operation Eagle Claw in 1980, the US Army decided to form its own dedicated special operations aviation regiment, the 160th SOAR. Known as the 'Night Stalkers', the 160th SOAR is responsible for supporting SOF personnel worldwide and is capable of carrying out a wide range of missions such as armed attack, force insertion and extraction, aerial security, electronic warfare and command and control support.

Pilots serving in the 160th SOAR are among the best in the world and train constantly to keep up their proficiency. Since their formation the 160th have seen action in Grenada, Panama, Iran, the Gulf, Somalia and Afghanistan and their motto is ' Night Stalkers don't quit'.

The 160th SOAR operates some of the most sophisticated helicopters in the

A USAF SOG pilot lines up his PAVE low for a top-up.

world including the A/MH-6 Little Bird, used for short range infiltration/exfiltration, reconnaissance, re-supply, liaison duties and light strike; MH-60 K/L Blackhawk, used for medium range day and night insertion/extraction missions, re-supply, MEDEVAC, rescue and recovery and short range CSAR; MH-47 D/E Chinook, used for medium to long range all weather infiltration/exfiltration missions, refuelling operations, rescue and recovery missions and re-supply missions in hostile areas.

JOHN F. KENNEDY SPECIAL WARFARE CENTER AND SCHOOL

This facility is responsible for developing doctrine, running training courses for Army Special Forces in civil affairs, psychological operations, escape and evasion, survival and resistance to interrogation.

AIR FORCE SPECIAL OPERATIONS COMMAND (AFSOC)

AFSOC was established on 22 May 1990, and is America's specialized air power, capable of delivering special operations combat power 'anytime, anywhere'. AFSOC comprises some 10,000 personnel, of which twenty-two per cent are based overseas. AFSOC's aircrew are highly trained professionals that operate with cool, calm precision and are amongst the most respected aviators in the world today. The unit is capable of rapid deployment at short notice and operates with some of the best rotary and fixed wing aircraft available, giving SOF mobility, forward presence and engagement precision.

AFSOC has the following active Air National Guard (ANG) and Air Force Reserve units assigned to it:

16th Special Operations Wing (SOW) operates with eight special operations squadrons - five fixed wing, one rotary wing, an aviation foreign internal defence (FID) unit and a fixed-wing training squadron.

352nd and 353rd Special Operations Groups are based in the UK and Japan and have a theatre orientated group that comprises two fixed wing and one rotary wing special operations squadrons plus a special tactics squadron.

919th AF Reserve Special Operations Wing with two fixed wing special operations squadrons.

193rd Special Operations Wing (ANG) with one fixed wing special operations squadron.

720th Special Tactics Group

18th Flight Test Squadron

The Air Force Special Operations School

A USAF CSAR team practices a mock rescue of a downed pilot. In Iraq they would have done this for real, deep behind enemy lines and flying at low altitudes.

16TH SPECIAL OPERATIONS WING

This is the oldest unit in AFSOC and is responsible for deploying specially trained and equipped forces from each service on national security objectives. The wing focuses on unconventional warfare, including counter-insurgency and psychological operations during low intensity conflicts. It also provides precise, reliable and timely support to SOF worldwide. The squadron operates a mix of aircraft types.

720TH SPECIAL TACTICS GROUP

This unit has special operations combat controllers and para-rescue men who work jointly in special tactics teams. Their mission includes air traffic control for establishing air assault landing zones, close air support for strike aircraft and gunship missions, establishing casualty collection stations and providing trauma care for injured personnel.

SPECIAL OPERATIONS SCHOOL

The school provides special operations related education to personnel from all branches of the Department of Defense, governmental agencies and allied nations. Subjects covered include regional affairs and cross cultural communications, anti-terrorism awareness, revolutionary warfare and psychological operations.

JOINT SPECIAL OPERATIONS COMMAND (JSOC)

JSOC was established in 1980. It is a joint headquarters designed to study special operations requirements and techniques, ensure interoperability and equipment standardization, plan and conduct special operations exercises and training and develop joint special operations tactics.

NAVAL SPECIAL WARFARE COMMAND

Naval Special Warfare Command was formed on 16 April 1987, at Naval Amphibious Base Coronado in San Diego, California. It is the naval component of Special Operations Command which is located in Tampa, Florida, and its mission is to both prepare Naval Special Warfare (NSW) forces for their assigned missions and to develop special operations strategy, doctrine and tactics.

Naval Special Warfare Command has operational control and responsibility for the administration, maintenance, training, support and readiness of all active-duty and reserve NSW personnel. The most significant operational components of Naval Special Warfare Command include Naval Special Warfare Group One and Special Boat Squadron One in San Diego and Special Warfare Group Two and Special Boat Squadron Two in Norfolk, Virginia. They deploy

A SEAL team member suspended from a helicopter over the flight deck of a US carrier.

SEAL teams, SEAL Delivery Vehicle Teams and Special Boat Units all over the world in support of operational exercises and both the training and wartime requirements of theatre commanders. With a force of some 5,000 active duty personnel which includes 2,200 SEALS and 600 Special Warfare Combatant-craft crewmen (SWCC), Naval Special Warfare Command is a highly potent force. Its missions include unconventional warfare, special reconnaissance, direct action, foreign internal defence, information warfare, security assistance, counter-drug operations, personnel recovery, hydrographic reconnaissance and counter-terrorism. NSW is a tactical force with strategic impact and,

A student undergoing weapons training at Special Operations School.

although it accounts for less than one per cent of US Navy personnel, it offers 'big bangs for little bucks'.

SEALS can operate both conventionally and unconventionally and have proved themselves in numerous conflicts. Their ability to provide real time intelligence and eyes on the ground for targeting purposes means that military planners can now make far better informed decisions on their use of tactical assets and in any future conflict that is an envious capability to have.

The most important trait of Navy SEALS is that they are a maritime force that strikes from the sea and returns to the sea and the name SEALS reflects the elements from which they operate, (sea, air, land). Their stealthy and clandestine methods of operation allow them to conduct multiple missions against targets that larger forces would have difficulty approaching undetected.

Naval Special Warfare Command is made up as follows:

Naval Special Warfare Command
Commander Naval Special Warfare Group One (CNSWG-1)

Group One Det Training
Group One Logistics and Support Unit
Group One Logistics and Support Unit CSST
Naval Special Warfare Unit One (NSWU-1)
Naval Special Warfare Unit Three (NSWU-3)
SEAL Team One (ST-1)
SEAL Team Three (ST-3)
SEAL Team Five (ST-5)
SEAL Team Seven (ST-7)

Commander Naval Special Warfare Group Two (CNSWG-2)

Group Two Det Training
Group Two Logistics and Support Unit
Group Two Logistics and Support Unit CSST
Naval Special Warfare Unit Two (NSWU-2)
Naval Special Warfare Unit Four (NSWU-4)
Naval Special Warfare Unit Ten (NSWU-10)

SEAL Team Two (ST-2)
SEAL TEAM Four (ST-4)
SEAL Team Eight (ST-8)
SEAL Team Ten (ST-10)

Commander Naval Special Warfare Group Three (CNSWG-3)
Special Boat Team Twelve (SBT-12)
SEAL Delivery Vehicle Team One (SDVT-1)
SEAL Delivery Vehicle Team One ASDS

Commander Naval Special Warfare Group Four (CNSWG-4)
Special Boat Team Twenty (SBT-20)
Special Boat Team Twenty Det Caribbean
Special Boat Team Twenty Two (SBT-22)
Special Boat Team Twenty Two Det Sacramento

SEAL Delivery Vehicle Team Two (SDVT-2)
Naval Special Warfare Center (NSWC)
Naval Special Warfare Center SDV Training Det Panama City
Naval Special Warfare Center Training Det Key West
Naval Special Warfare Center Advanced Training Det Little Creek
Naval Special Warfare Center Det Hawaii

COALITION COMMAND & CONTROL
THE UK'S
SAS ORGANIZATION

SPECIAL FORCES GROUP
CO: Brigadier

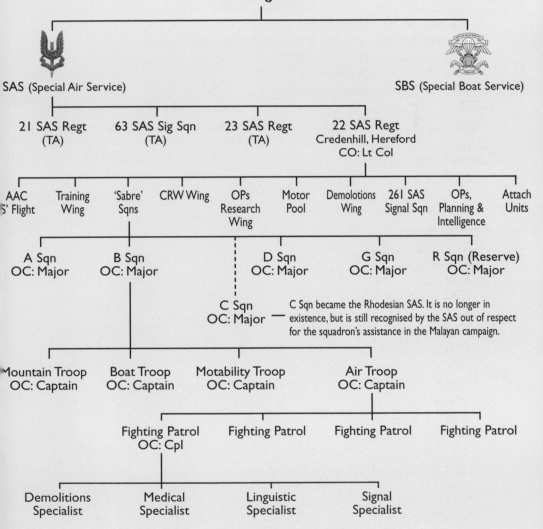

SAS (Special Air Service)

SBS (Special Boat Service)

21 SAS Regt (TA)

63 SAS Sig Sqn (TA)

23 SAS Regt (TA)

22 SAS Regt
Credenhill, Hereford
CO: Lt Col

AAC 'S' Flight

Training Wing

'Sabre' Sqns

CRW Wing

OPs Research Wing

Motor Pool

Demolitions Wing

261 SAS Signal Sqn

OPs, Planning & Intelligence

Attach Units

A Sqn
OC: Major

B Sqn
OC: Major

D Sqn
OC: Major

G Sqn
OC: Major

R Sqn (Reserve)
OC: Major

C Sqn
OC: Major

C Sqn became the Rhodesian SAS. It is no longer in existence, but is still recognised by the SAS out of respect for the squadron's assistance in the Malayan campaign.

Mountain Troop
OC: Captain

Boat Troop
OC: Captain

Motability Troop
OC: Captain

Air Troop
OC: Captain

Fighting Patrol
OC: Cpl

Fighting Patrol

Fighting Patrol

Fighting Patrol

Demolitions Specialist

Medical Specialist

Linguistic Specialist

Signal Specialist

Naval Special Warfare Center Det Yuma
Naval Special Warfare Center Det Hurlburt
Naval Special Warfare Center Det Kodiak
Naval Small Craft Instruction and Technical Training School (NAVSCIATTS)

 ## AUSTRALIA'S SPECIAL OPERATIONS COMMAND

Established in May 2003 and headed by Major General Duncan Lewis it comprises:

A joint HQ with offices in both Canberra and Sydney
The **Special Air Service Regiment (SASR)**
The **4th Battalion, the Royal Australian Regiment** (Commando)
The **Tactical Assault Group** (West) and (East)
The **1st Commando Regiment**
The **Incident Response Regiment**

The Special Operations Service Support Company is a unit that comprises logistics, communications, heavy weapons and a Special Forces aviation support element, operated and manned by 330 highly trained personnel that are available to supplement Australia's existing Special Forces ORBAT in an emergency.

An Australian trooper of 4RAR, patrols the desert in Iraq.

CHAPTER SIX

SPECIAL FORCES: SELECTION AND TRAINING

USA - DELTA FORCE

'These are guys that are putting their lives on the line, taking on some very serious bad guys. The less anyone knows about the unit, the better.'

Former Delta Force soldier quoted in *Stars and Stripes*.

Colonel Charles Beckwith served in the British SAS and liked it so much that he formed his own version: Delta Force. Although very similar to the SAS in training and operational capability when first formed in 1977, Delta now has its own exacting and demanding standards and they are very tough.

Unlike the US Navy SEALS, who are very open and frank about their selection and training process for potential operators, Delta is completely the opposite and discusses little or nothing about its requirements. However what is known about Delta is that twice a year representatives from the unit make a trip to the Army's main personnel centre in St Louis, Missouri, to examine soldiers' military records. Their mission is to find outstanding captains and sergeants among the Green Berets and Rangers who have skills that are of interest to Delta. The soldiers they have selected are sent letters telling them that Delta is interested in them. There is a telephone number for them to call if the feeling is mutual. However if the answer is negative, they are instructed to destroy the letter.

For those that make the call, an interview follows which quickly weeds out unsuitable candidates. Potential candidates are then subjected to a tough PT test that is more demanding than the normal army test. Those that pass who are not already parachute qualified must undertake a course at an airborne school

US soldiers undergoing rigorous training, designed to test physical endurance.

before they can go any further. Before commencing selection, each soldier is put through an intensive week of PT that involves running, swimming and forced marches with heavy packs. The idea behind this PT week is that it gives candidates a chance to improve their physical fitness and also highlights any injuries or medical issues that need to be addressed before selection proper.

Once through these initial hurdles the candidates go to Camp Dawson, an Army National Guard post in West Virginia's Appalachian Mountains for a one month selection and assessment phase. This part of the course is very similar to that of the British SAS as Delta's founder, Colonel Beckwith, felt it was the best in the world for sorting the wheat from the chaff. Like SAS selection, only a small percentage of each intake passes; in most cases this number rarely gets into double figures.

Typically, during selection, candidates are subjected to long marches with heavy packs, over areas that are both mentally and physically demanding. They are never given timings or any information regarding their progress and they don't know, from one day to the next, whether they are in or out.

Delta's original selection course was modelled on that of the British SAS; however over the years it has been slightly changed to better reflect American requirements in relation to course health and safety issues.

One of the toughest aspects of selection for candidates is the isolation factor, as they have little contact with anyone, apart from the instructors. For many candidates this a difficult concept for them to deal with as they are used to working as part of a team and the whole idea of being a loner goes against the grain. This is the exact purpose of the exercise as Delta wants operators that can react quickly to change.

One of the most interesting and controversial aspects of Delta's selection process is the psychological examination that each candidate must undergo before being considered as a potential operator, or 'D' man. During the psychological phase, candidates are subjected to a barrage of questions and demands from a number of different doctors:

Describe your relationship with your family.
Do you like foreigners?
Do you take drugs?
Are you running away from something?
How do you feel about gays in the Army?
Do you feel that you are ugly?
Do you look in the mirror and see Rambo?
Are you scared of the dark?

The questioning is relentless as the doctors want to build up a detailed psychological profile of each candidate. It is vital that they weed out any potential psychopaths and prevent them from entering Delta's ranks.

The ideal candidate is a stable individual who has an emotional anchor in his or her life such as a family or religion, as they tend to be the most reliable soldiers. What Delta doesn't want are loner types as they rarely fit in and definitely no one with criminal tendencies. The other key area of a candidate's profile that greatly concerns Delta, relates to his or her ability to handle extreme stress situations while carrying a gun. What Delta is looking for is a fine balance between someone who is willing to pull a trigger, yet is not too hesitant either.

After completion of the psychological evaluation each candidate is asked to write a short autobiography that must be frank and honest.

During the second week of the pre-selection phase, candidates are physically worn down by seemingly endless forced marches that eventually end with a tough eighteen mile march at night through dense woodland. The idea behind this phase is to exhaust candidates before they begin the next eighteen days of

The stresses and strains of a forced march begin to take their toll on these soldiers.

formal selection.

As the candidates begin the formal part of selection they are given a number and a colour. The number identifies the individual and the colour designates their squad. They are not allowed to talk to other candidates, and the Delta instructors say little to them as individuals. When addressing the candidates the instructors are very matter of fact and do not engage them in conversation, nor do they give them any clue as to how they are doing. The instructors never shout at the candidates, and never praise them either. They don't frown and don't smile, which often unnerves the candidate as they have no idea of their progress at any given time.

A typical day begins with a self wake-up at 6 a.m. as there is no reveille. Within each barrack room is a blackboard with the day's instructions written on it - Red 3 report to vehicle 6 at 07.00 hrs with full kit and a 40 pound pack - for example.

Every day the reporting times differ, as do the weights, with no two days being alike. Even during the day the weights can be changed, sometimes in the candidate's favour but mostly not. Any candidates found with underweight packs are punished on the spot by instructors who give them a heavy rock to carry.

Generally candidates receive two hot meals a day, one in the morning and one at night, but at some point they will get nothing as the instructors want to see which candidates have prepared for such an event.

A typical candidate's march will start with a truck picking him up shortly after breakfast and dropping him off on a back road somewhere in the forest as part of a small four man group. He will then be given a point on a map and told to get there as quickly as possible. As he makes his way towards the check point, he has no idea of what the expected reporting time is and this will play on his mind throughout the journey. Once he arrives at the check point he will be tired, blistered and anxious, as he will not know if he has passed or failed this particular exercise. The impassive instructors give nothing away as they mark their notebooks and only speak to advise the candidate of his next check point. As for the candidate, he just has to keep going until he reaches the next check point where he will hopefully get some food and rest. Before bedding down he will be given a time for meeting up with the rest of the cadre next morning. However, if he oversleeps there will be nobody to wake him up and, should this happen, he will miss the truck and fail selection.

Throughout the next few days the routine varies from eight hours of marching with three MRE (Meals Ready to Eat) packets, to thirty-six hours of marching with only one MRE. To help in disorientating the candidate, his number and colours are changed on a fairly frequent basis so he never really feels safe or secure. At any point he can be stopped by an instructor and ordered to strip and reassemble a foreign weapon, while being asked difficult mathematical questions. On occasions he will be approached by doctors who

Delta Force operatives have to become familiar with the operation and use of foreign weapons. This soldier carries the Russian made AK-47 during an exercise.

briefly observe and scribble notes without saying a word. Little does the candidate know that at some point or other he will be photographed by Delta instructors who want to make sure that he is ploughing his way through the woodland and not cheating by using the paths. If caught once by the instructors on a path or road, he will receive an official warning; caught twice and he is out.

For many of the candidates the stress is just too much for them and they quit, while for others they have already failed but just don't know it yet. To help sow confusion in the cadre, instructors often place failed candidates within their ranks so they have no way of gauging the general standards of the other candidates.

Every candidate is allowed a number of lives, but they are never told how many of them they have left or indeed how many they had when they started out. If a soldier drops out or is failed during selection, he receives a pep talk from the Delta instructors who praise his efforts and point out his good points, as well as his bad. They try to let the failed candidates down as softly as possible as they don't want to damage his confidence or future career. In addition to the talk, Delta also makes a point of writing to the candidate's parent unit and thanking them for providing a good soldier that is a credit to his unit. This process may seem a little over the top but it is done for the very good reason that one day Delta may need the support of this soldier during an operation and they want no ill feelings that could cause possible friction.

When a candidate is failed during selection, there is no scene or melodrama. They are simply whisked away without the other candidates ever being told why. For most candidates each day that goes by is a victory for them, as many of their fellow cadre members will have been either failed or dismissed by now, leaving only about twenty per cent of the original intake left for the final phase.

The last phase of selection involves a march of forty miles in two days along the open and winding Appalachian Trail with full kit. It is a very difficult march that breaks many of the candidates, but for those that pass this gruelling event, a hot meal and a warm shower await them back at the base camp.

Once back at the barracks the remaining candidates are given a number of books to read that are intellectually challenging. They then have just eighteen hours in which to write a detailed report on the contents of each book. The instructors set this exercise as a means of evaluating how alert the candidates are after two days without sleep. After handing in their reports, the candidates are subjected to a further series of interviews in which they have to answer questions on their childhood, family, military career and the selection course itself. Those that survive this interview move on to the final hurdle, the commander's board. During this interview the candidate sits in a chair surrounded by Delta's commander and his five squadron leaders. The board reads through all of the candidate's psychiatric reports and starts asking difficult questions such as;

Would you give your child's life up for your country?
You are on a mission and a young shepherd stumbles across your hide; are you prepared to kill him?
You have been ordered by the President to kill one of his political rivals; are you willing to carry out this order?

The idea behind this questioning is to see how a candidate reacts to pressure from a higher authority. Does he get flustered easily? Does he panic while under pressure? Can he be trusted with secret information? and so on.

On some occasions during a board, a candidate will be asked if he cheated at any point on the course by using roads or paths. If he did and admits to it he may be kept on. However if he lies about cheating, photographic proof will be shown to him that will result in his instant dismissal.

After the candidate's interview is over, the senior Delta officers meet in private to discuss him. All aspects of his performance throughout the selection process are evaluated and if there are still any lingering doubts about anyone at this stage they are rejected. Technically, Delta's commander can overrule any rejection decision; however he rarely does. The decision to accept a candidate is made by majority vote only.

Once a candidate is accepted into Delta, his selection and assessment reports are sealed for eternity and no one, including the candidate, is allowed to see the scores or, indeed, know what the pass mark was on this selection course.

After passing selection the candidate is sent on the Operators' Training Course, which consists of six months of instruction in covert operations, commando assaults, CQB and sniping.

The pace of the OTC is relaxed compared with that of selection but there is still a formal air to the course as all new students are on probation for the first year. A typical training course sees students spending over 1,000 hours in the Delta shooting house alone, where they will learn about every aspect of combat shooting until it becomes second nature.

In addition to the practical exercises, students attend numerous lectures on subjects such as psychology, combat theory, world politics and terrorism. However, it's not all dull and boring as the students also learn how to ride motor

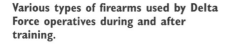

Various types of firearms used by Delta Force operatives during and after training.

bikes as part of vehicle familiarization training. The students also receive detailed instruction on clandestine operations and image projection - how to dress while working undercover.

After this phase is over the students spend six weeks studying communications, combat medicine and advanced infantry skills, followed by nine weeks of assault and rescue operation training that includes two and four man assaults, how to enter buildings, rope- work and helicopter insertion. The

Tactical weapons training and HALO/HAHO parachute infiltration are all part of a Delta Force operator's tasks.

students then work with the CIA on real tasks such as VIP protection and intelligence gathering operations, which are usually carried out against low level criminals.

Once they have finished this training they move onto what Delta Force is really all about, as they are now trained operators. Even though the formal aspect of training is over, there will always be other courses in subjects such as EOD, scuba and HALO/HAHO parachute infiltration.

In addition to their training in the United States, Delta operators frequently cross-train with other counter-terrorist units around the world including the German GSG-9, French GIGN, Australian SASR and, of course, the British SAS with whom they work very closely.

Delta Force is organized along the same lines as the British SAS and consists

A Delta Force operator is expected to undergo scuba diving training, not to mention mountain and arctic warfare training.

Delta operators frequently cross-train with foreign forces and other counter-terrorist units. Above right: A member of the much feared and respected German GSG-9, a unit with which Delta operators often work.

of three operating squadrons, (A, B and C) which are subdivided into smaller units known as troops. Each troop specializes in a particular skill such as mountaineering, HALO, scuba or Land mobility. For greater operational efficiency each troop can be divided into smaller four-man units that can either operate alone or join up to form a section.

Delta also has its own support squadron which handles selection and training, logistics, finance, technical and medical issues. The technical unit is of particular interest as it provides Delta with highly sensitive equipment such as human tracking devices and eavesdropping sensors which are used during hostage rescue operations.

Delta operators also enjoy some of the best training facilities in the world and have access to an Olympic-sized swimming pool, diving tank and a three-storey climbing wall as well as numerous shooting ranges that include a CQB and sniping facility.

The vast majority of Delta's recruits come from the elite Ranger and Airborne battalions. However a significant number of potential candidates also come from conventional Army units, including the Army Reserve and National Guard.

DELTA FORCE OFFICER REQUIRMENTS

Joining a Special Forces unit as an ordinary soldier is hard enough but becoming an officer is something else, as every man or woman must possess the exceptional qualities needed to lead the best of the best.

Shown here are the requirements for becoming an officer in the US Army's 1st Special Forces Operational Detachment - Delta (1st-SFOD).

OPPORTUNITIES

Officer Assignment Opportunities in Delta Force
(Taken from: US Army PERSCOM Online)

The U.S. Army's 1st Special Forces Operational Detachment - Delta (1st SFOD) plans and conducts a broad range of special operations across the operational continuum. Delta is organized for the conduct of missions requiring rapid response with surgical applications of a wide variety of unique skills, while maintaining the lowest possible profile of U.S. involvement.

Assignment to 1st SFOD-D involves an extensive pre-screening process, successful completion of a three to four week mentally and physically demanding assessment and selection course, and a six month operator training course. Upon successful completion of these courses, officers are assigned to an operational position within the unit.

As an officer in 1st SFOD-D, you will have added opportunities to command at the captain, major and lieutenant colonel levels. You may also serve as an Operations Officer. After service with 1st SFOD-D there are a wide variety of staff positions available to you at DOD, JCS, DA, USASOC, USSOCOM and Joint Headquarters because of your training and experience. In addition, there are interagency positions available to you as well.

The prerequisites for an officer are:

Male
Volunteer
US Citizen
Pass a modified Class II Flight Physical
Airborne qualified or volunteer for airborne training
Pass a background security investigation and have at least a secret clearance
Pass the Army Physical Fitness Test (APFT), FM 21-20, 75 points each event in the 22-26 age group, (55 push-ups in two minutes, 62 sit-ups in two minutes and a 2 mile run in 15:06 or less), wearing your unit PT uniform.
Minimum of two years active service remaining upon selection into the unit.
Captain or Major (Branch immaterial)
Advance course graduate
College graduate (BA or BS)
Minimum of 12 months successful command (as a Captain)

1st SFOD-D conducts worldwide recruiting twice a year to process potential candidates for the assessment and selection course. Processing for the September course is from October to January. Processing for the September course takes place from April to July.

Assignments with 1st SFOD-D provide realistic training and experiences that are both personally and professionally rewarding.

UK - SAS (SPECIAL AIR SERVICE)

The British SAS have one of the most demanding selection courses in the world that is designed to challenge a candidate both physically and mentally to the point of absolute exhaustion as this is the only way to judge if a candidate has the right aptitude for SAS training. The regular SAS Regiment only considers applicants who are already serving in the British Army and have completed at least three years' of service. However the TA (Territorial Army Reserve Force) SAS accepts potential candidates from both serving members of the reserve forces and outside civilian volunteers. They are looking for men that have physical and mental strength, initiative, self-reliance and the intelligence to work through highly complex issues while exhausted and under extreme stress. The selection process is designed to weed out the unsuitable as soon as possible, as there are always dreamers and time wasters who apply for SAS service without realizing what is actually required of them. Typical candidates are generally in their mid-twenties although older applicants do apply for selection.

Selection courses are run twice a year, once in summer and once in winter and candidates have no choice of which one they attend. There are many schools of thought on which one is the easier to pass, as both have their good and bad points. However the ratio of success on both courses is more or less the same.

An SAS candidate stops to take a compass bearing during selection.

It is assumed that if a man feels confident enough to apply for the SAS, then he must also appreciate the physical and mental tasks that lie ahead for him and must prepare for them as best he can. The Selection Training programme lasts for one month and is run by the Training Wing of 22 SAS at Credenhill, Hereford. The selection programme was originally designed in 1953 and has changed very little over the years, as it is a tried and tested system.

It commences with a build-up period of two weeks for officers and three weeks for all other ranks. The reason why the officers' work up period is shorter than the other ranks is because SAS officers are expected to out-perform their men in every aspect of military knowledge and skills; otherwise they have no business being officers in this regiment.

To attend selection all candidates must undergo a medical at their parent unit and must be certified fit by their regimental medical officer. Before the candidates commence selection they are given a chance to work up their strength as some of them may have been on operational tours where they will have had little time to prepare. Therefore during the first week of selection candidates start the course with a series of training

The Brecon Beacons in South Wales; the back breaking amd treacherous terrain all SAS candidates have to endure in the early part of selection.

runs that get progressively longer each day. Each candidate must be capable of passing the standard Battle Fitness test (BFT) in the same time as an average infantryman; anything longer and he will fail selection. As the selection programme continues, the candidates are sent on a series of long, hard, forced marches over the Brecon Beacons and Black Mountains of South Wales. The marches are designed to test their navigation and map reading skills as well as their physical strength. The marches place relentless demands on the candidates as they are given ever more complex and daunting problems to solve by day and night in all weathers, carrying a pack that starts off weighing twenty-four pounds (eleven kilos) and by the end of the week will increase to fifty-five pounds (twenty-five kilos). During the winter months these mountains are often covered in mist and snow, making navigation extremely difficult as the candidates cannot see visual reference points. The winds blowing over the mountains can frequently reach gale force making it very difficult for a man to stand upright, let alone walk. Another problem for the candidates is the ground itself, particularly if it has been raining hard, as it will become very marshy, making the going very tough indeed. Although Selection is designed to test candidates to their physical limits, there are frequent checkpoints throughout the route that candidates must pass through. These checkpoints serve three purposes; they prevent cheating, they provide information about the candidates' next route and they ensure the candidates' safety as there have been numerous fatalities over the years on the Brecon Beacons, mainly from hypothermia and severe falls. At one stage the SAS even trialled satellite tracking devices as an additional safety measure.

Throughout selection the emphasis is on the individual candidate and not the entire cadre, which generally numbers 120 men. Each candidate must rely on himself for motivation as the instructors are not there to help or indeed hinder them; they are there for providing information and safety cover only. At no time will they give a candidate any indication of how he is doing or how much time he has left to complete a task. Throughout selection, candidates voluntarily drop out or are told that they have failed. Indeed for many of the candidates it is only when they report for the next march and see their name on the instructor's list that they know they are still OK. For those that are not on the list, a short journey back to the base camp awaits them where they will be thanked for attempting selection and given a travel warrant back to their respective unit. Some of the candidates will be given a second chance to attempt selection, but for most this will be the end of the line for them. The SAS makes a point of talking to those that have failed selection to reassure them that they are still good soldiers and that they have many good qualities, but not the ones they require.

As the remaining candidates ponder their fate each morning, they take some comfort from the fact that they are still in the programme and a day closer to passing selection. As each day begins the candidates are given a new route and a series of RV points that they must make in order to gain further information. They are not allowed to write anything down and are forbidden to mark their maps in any way as this could give away valuable information. Since they are on their own at all times and have no idea of timings from checkpoint to checkpoint they just have to push as hard and as fast as they can until they are told to stop by the instructors.

On occasions the instructors will order a candidate to stop and strip his weapon down and then reassemble it again. They usually pick a time when the candidate is clearly cold and exhausted and therefore vulnerable, as his coordination will be slower than normal.

One favourite trick of the instructors' is to place a map and a magnetic compass on a metal bonnet of a vehicle so that it distorts its reading. They then brief the candidates around the vehicle and issue them with a new bearing to march on. However, once the compass is lifted from the bonnet the bearing will change quite significantly and if the candidates fail to pick up on this point they are likely to get lost.

During one exercise on the final week of selection, the instructors take away the maps from the candidates and provide them instead with poorly drawn sketch maps that have little on them apart from a few marked points. The candidates then have to use all of their navigational skills to find the checkpoints that will provide the missing data. On another exercise known as the 'Fan Dance' the candidates have to negotiate an extremely difficult geographical feature known as Pen-Y-Fan (or 'The Fan' as the SAS often call it) three times in four hours from three different points. However at no point are they told about the number of times they will be required to climb the 2,900 feet peak or how much time has been allocated for the task. All of the climbs are very difficult, especially when carrying a heavy pack and a rifle and it comes as no surprise that this exercise is the most demanding on the selection phase.

As the selection phase reaches its climax, the candidates are marching all day and even through most of the night, ending on the final day with a fifty-mile

Candidates are expected to walk over high and treacherous terrain carrying a fifty-five pound pack and a rifle, while exhausted, in less than twenty hours.

march across the Brecon Beacons. This march includes 'The Fan' and other local geographical nasties. An average person walks at a pace of two to three miles per hour on flat ground. These men have to walk over very high and treacherous terrain carrying a fifty-five pound pack (twenty-five kilos) and a rifle, while exhausted, in less than twenty hours. It is a daunting task to say the least. Needless to say, the failure rate during the selection phase is very high indeed with, on average, only seven to fifteen per cent of each cadre completing it successfully.

For those few that pass the selection phase the worst is yet to come, as they now go into a six month training period known simply as continuation. The first phase of continuation lasts for fourteen weeks and is designed to teach new recruits basic SAS skills such as movement behind enemy lines, contact drills, signalling and the operational roles of the standard SAS four-man team.

All recruits have to reach basic signaller standard, regardless of their rank and future specialization, as communications play a key part in Special Forces operations. In addition to this training all recruits learn basic field medicine, sniping, ground control of air, mortar and artillery fire, survival skills, sabotage and demolition skills and foreign weapons handling.

After completing the skills phase of continuation, the recruit moves on to the combat and survival element of continuation that teaches new SAS members how to fight and survive behind enemy lines with little or no support. The recruits are taught how to find and build shelters, locate food and water and how to escape and evade enemy capture. Once this training is complete the recruits embark on a five-day escape and evasion exercise in the Brecon Beacons in which they have to evade capture from an enemy force. The enemy part is usually played by a local infantry battalion or, on occasions, a NATO battalion if any happen to be in the UK on exercise at the time. No matter how good the recruits are throughout the exercise, the instructors ensure that they are caught at some time or other as they cannot move forward without completing the Resistance to Interrogation (RTI) phase of continuation.

The RTI phase lasts for around twenty-four hours and is one of the harshest elements of continuation. It has to be, as the SAS must be sure of its men at all times as much of their work is behind enemy lines. The regiment has to be confident that they will not crack while working under pressure and betray their fellow operators and RTI is probably the best means of finding out if the SAS has a potential weak link. Much of the RTI phase is classified. However some aspects of it are public knowledge and it is clearly no secret that it is both physically and mentally challenging. Although no physical torture takes place during the RTI phase, there is no shortage of mind games that border on severe mental torture, as the instructors and expert interrogators do their utmost to unhinge the recruit. They have many ways of breaking a man down without so much as touching them.

This can be done in many ways including subjecting the recruit to constant deafening white noise that can sheer metal if the decibel level is high enough, blindfolding recruits and then handcuffing them to active railway lines and pouring petrol over them and leaving them near an open fire. Again, it must be stressed that no physical harm comes to recruits from these methods, and many people may well ask, why does the SAS subject its men to such barbaric treatment in this day and age? There is a very simple answer; it works.

After the RTI phase is over, recruits are sent on a jungle survival course that lasts for up to six weeks. This course is normally held in the Far East, usually in Brunei, and trains recruits in survival, building shelters, finding food and water, navigation and jungle warfare. The SAS has fought many of its most remarkable campaigns in the jungle in places such as Malaya and Borneo and places great emphasis on its jungle warfare training.

Those that pass the jungle phase move to RAF Brize Norton in Oxfordshire to undergo parachute training with No.1 Parachute Training School. As many of the regiment's new recruits are ex-paras, they are excused this course. However the others will have to undergo four weeks of static-line training, followed by eight jumps, that includes one at night.

After passing parachute training the recruits are awarded their 'Sabre' wings and on return to Hereford they are presented with their sand coloured beret, complete with winged dagger cap badge. They are now members of the Special Air Service Regiment and regardless of their previous rank they revert to the lowest rank in the SAS which is that of trooper, but continue to be paid according to their previous rank. Even though they have been accepted into the SAS, they

The toughest beret to receive in the British Army, the 'winged dagger' beret.

A soldier during a HAHO airborne exercise. Right: Jungle training under dense canopy.

The various skills of the SAS soldier.

are on probation for their first year and can still be dismissed at any point during this time.

The new soldiers are assigned to one of 22 SAS Regiment's squadrons and have a choice between joining Boat, Air, Mountain or Mobility Troop. Those selecting Boat Troop learn about maritime operations and how to handle small boats such as rigid raiders, kayaks and submersibles. Troopers also undergo scuba and specialist diving training that includes underwater demolition and maritime counter-terrorist operations.

Troopers joining Air Troop undergo specialist training in HALO/HAHO techniques both in the UK and overseas. In addition they learn all aspects of airborne insertion, conventional and unconventional, including the use of heavily modified long range helicopters.

Those that join Mountain Troop learn about mountain and arctic warfare, including survival training, climbing techniques and the use of equipment such as skis, sledges and skidoos.

Troopers joining Mobility Troop train in vehicle operation both in conventional and unconventional roles such as deep reconnaissance and hit and run type missions for which the SAS is renowned. Troopers learn how to drive defensively and offensively in different types of terrain ranging from woodland to desert and practise ambush and counter-ambush techniques until they are second nature.

At some point each trooper will rotate through counter-terrorist training, as the SAS is the UK's primary counter-terrorist unit. Training includes CQB, sniping, fast-roping, insertion techniques, tubular work and unarmed combat.

Since the SAS is the world's most feared and respected Special Forces unit, there are many opportunities for troopers to cross-train with other units around the world such as the US Delta Force, German GSG-9 and KSK, and both the Australian and New Zealand SAS.

CHAPTER SEVEN

SPECIAL & ELITE FORCES INVOLVED IN OPERATION IRAQI FREEDOM

UK FORCES INVOLVED IN OPERATION IRAQI FREEDOM

ROYAL NAVY - Rear Admiral David Snelson

HMS *Ark Royal* (aircraft carrier)
HMS *Ocean* (helicopter carrier)
HMS *Edinburgh* (Type 42 destroyer)
HMS *Liverpool* (Type 42 destroyer)
HMS *York* (Type 42)
HMS *Marlborough* (Type 23 frigate)
HMS *Richmond* (Type 23 frigate)
HMS *Chatham* (Type 22 frigate)
HMS *Grimsby* (minehunter)
HMS *Ledbury* (minehunter)
HMS *Brocklesby* (minehunter)
HMS *Blyth* (minehunter)
HMS *Splendid* (Swiftsure class submarine)
HMS *Turbulent* (Trafalgar class submarine)
RFA *Argus*
RFA *Sir Galahad*
RFA *Sir Tristram*
RFA *Sir Percivale*
RFA *Fort Victoria*
RFA *Fort Rosalie*
RFA *Fort Austin*
RFA *Orangeleaf*

ROYAL MARINES AMPHIBIOUS FORCE - Commodore Jamie Miller

comprising some 4,000 personnel from

HQ 3 Commando Brigade

Brigadier Jim Dutton

40 Commando Royal Marines

42 Commando Royal Marines

45 Commando Royal Marines

29 Regiment, Royal Artillery (equipped with 105mm light guns)

539 Assault Squadron, RM

59 Commando Squadron, RE

Plus elements of the SBS (Special Boat Service)

Helicopter air groups deployed on board HMS *Ark Royal* and HMS *Ocean*: 845, 846, 847, and 849 Squadrons.

Royal Marines train for the fight ahead. Note the variety of weaponry and equipment at their disposal.

Royal Marines in
the fight for Iraq.

ARMY - Major General Robin Brims
(UK) Armoured Division:
Headquarters and 1 Armoured Division Signal Regiment
30 Signal Regiment (strategic communications)
The Queens Dragon Guards (reconnaissance)
1st Battalion the Duke of Wellington's Regiment (additional infantry support)
28 Engineer Regiment
1 General Support Regiment, Royal Logistics Corps
2 Close Support Regiment, Royal Logistics Corps
2nd Battalion, Royal Electrical and Mechanical Engineers
1 Close Support Medical Regiment
5 General Support Medical Regiment
1 Regiment, Royal Military Police
plus elements from:
30 Signal Regiment
33 EOD Regiment
32 Regiment Royal Artillery (equipped with Phoenix UAVs)
7 Armoured Brigade
Brigadier Graham Binns
Headquarters and Signal Squadron
Royal Scots Dragoon Guards (equipped with Challenger 2 tanks)
2 Royal Tank Regiment (equipped with Challenger 2 tanks)
1st Battalion the Black Watch (equipped with Warrior Infantry Fighting Vehicles)
1st Battalion Royal Regiment of Fusiliers (equipped with Warrior Infantry Fighting Vehicles)
3 Regiment Royal Horse Artillery (equipped with AS90 self-propelled guns)
32 Armoured Engineer Regiment
plus various elements from other units including:
Queen's Royal Lancers (equipped with Challenger 2 tanks)
1st Battalion Irish Guards (equipped with Warrior Infantry Fighting Vehicles)
1st Battalion The Light Infantry (equipped with Warrior Infantry Fighting Vehicles)
26 Regiment Royal Artillery
38 Engineer Regiment
16 Air Assault Brigade
Brigadier Jacko Page
Headquarters and Signal Squadron
1st Battalion the Royal Irish Regiment
1st Battalion the Parachute Regiment
3rd Battalion the Parachute Regiment
7 (Para) Regiment Royal Horse Artillery (equipped with 105mm light guns)

23 Engineer Regiment
D Squadron, Household Cavalry Regiment
3 Regiment Army Air Corps (equipped with Lynx and Gazelle helicopters)
7th Air Assault Battalion, Royal Electrical and Mechanical Engineers
13 Air Assault Support Regiment, Royal Logistic Corps
16 Close Support Medical Regiment
156 Provost Company RMP
102 Logistics Brigade
Brigadier Shaun Cowlan
Headquarters 2 Signal Regiment
36 Engineering Regiment
33 and 34 Field Hospitals
202 Field Hospital (Volunteer)
General Support Medical Regiment
3rd Battalion, Royal Electrical and Mechanical Engineers
6 Supply Regiment, Royal Logistic Corps
7 Transport Regiment, Royal Logistic Corps
17 Port and Maritime Regiment, Royal Logistic Corps
23 Pioneer Regiment, Royal Logistic Corps
24 Regiment, Royal Logistic Corps
5 Regiment, Royal Military Police
plus additional support and specialist units from:
12 Engineer Brigade (airfield engineer support unit)
11 EOD Regiment
Royal Logistic Corps

Special Forces
22 SAS

ROYAL AIR FORCE - Air Vice Marshal Glenn Torpy

12, 14, 617 Squadrons, RAF Lossiemouth
11, 25 Squadrons, RAF Leeming
43, III Squadrons, RAF Leuchars
6, 41, IV Squadrons, RAF Cottesmore
8, 23, 51 Squadrons, RAF Waddington
33 Squadron, RAF Benson
10, 99 101,216 Squadrons, RAF Brize Norton
24, 30, 47, 70 Squadrons, RAF Lyneham
120, 201, 206 Squadrons, RAF Kinloss
7, 18, 27 Squadrons RAF Odiham
plus composite squadrons, formed from elements of
9, 13, 31, 39 (1 PRU) Squadrons, RAF Marham
RAF Regiment

Track bikes, ideal for scouting and recce type missions, as they rarely get bogged down in sand.

As good as Special Forces are, they still need conventional forces such as these fusiliers in southern Iraq.

A brace of RAF Tornado F3s fly a CAP in support of ground forces.

An RAF GR7 Harrier being bombed up for another mission over Iraq. At one stage they even operated out of a captured airbase in the western desert - a perfect example of expeditionary warfare.

AUSTRALIAN FORCES INVOLVED IN OPERATION IRAQI FREEDOM

NAVY

HMAS *Kanimbla*
HMAS *Anzac*
HMAS *Darwin*

AIR FORCE

One RAAF squadron (equipped with F/A 18 aircraft)
Three RAAF C-130 aircraft
Two P3C Orion aircraft

ARMY

Special Forces Task Group
including SAS and 4 Royal Australian Regiment

POLISH FORCES INVOLVED IN OPERATION IRAQI FREEDOM GROM (SPECIAL FORCES)

US FORCES INVOLVED IN OPERATION IRAQI FREEDOM

ARMY

Special Operations Command
5th Special Forces Group
75th Ranger Regiment
160th Special Operations Aviation Regiment
Delta Force (deployed with Task Force 20)
3rd Infantry Division
1st Battalion, 39th Field Artillery Regiment
11th Aviation Regiment
1st Brigade
2nd, 3rd Battalions, 7th Infantry Regiment
3rd Battalion, 69th Armor Regiment
1st Battalion, 41st Field Artillery Regiment
2nd Brigade
3rd Battalion, 15th Infantry Regiment
1st, 4th Battalions, 64th Armor Regiment
E Troop, 9th Cavalry Regiment
1st Battalion, 9th Field Artillery Regiment
3rd Brigade
1st Battalion, 30th Infantry Regiment
1st Battalion, 15th Infantry Regiment
2nd Battalion, 69th Armor Regiment
D Troop, 10th Cavalry Regiment

1st Battalion, 10th Field Artillery Regiment
Aviation Brigade
1st Battalion, 3rd Aviation Regiment
2nd Battalion, 3rd Aviation Regiment
3rd Squadron, 7th Cavalry Regiment
82nd Airborne Division
2nd Brigade Combat Team
1st, 2nd, 3rd Battalions, 325th Airborne Infantry
1st Battalion, 82nd Aviation Regiment
101st Airborne Division
1st Brigade, 101st Airborne Division
1st, 2nd, 3rd Battalions, 327th Infantry Regiment
2nd Brigade, 101st Airborne Division
1st, 2nd, 3rd Battalions, 502nd Infantry Regiment
3rd Brigade, 101st Airborne Division
1st, 2nd, 3rd Battalions, 187th Infantry Regiment

2nd Battalion, 17th Cavalry Regiment
1st, 2nd, 3rd, 6th Battalions, 101st Aviation Regiment
159th Aviation Brigade
4th, 5th, 7th, 9th Battalions, 101st Aviation Regiment
1st, 2nd, 3rd Battalions,
320th Field Artillery Regiment
173rd Airborne Brigade
1st, 2nd Battalions, 508th Infantry
173rd Engineer Detachment
173rd Brigade Recon Company
Battery D, 3rd Battalion, 319th Airborne Field Artillery

MARINE CORPS
MARINE EXPEDITIONARY FORCE

1st Marine Division
1st Marine Regiment
3rd Battalion, 1st Marines
1st Battalion, 4th Marines
1st, 3rd Battalions, light Armored Recon
5th Marine Regiment
1st Battalion, 5th Marines
2nd, 3rd Battalions, 5th Marines
7th Marine Regiment
1st, 3rd Battalions, 7th Marines
3rd Battalion, 4th Marines
3rd Battalion, 11th Marines
1st Tank Battalion

An Australian operator passes two ships of the desert prior to Operation Iraqi Freedom.

An Australian F/A-18 Hornet pilot prepares for a mission over Iraq.

Looking mean and moody, an operator from 4 RAR poses for the camera.

A US Airborne soldier provides cover for his buddies in northern Iraq following an air drop.

Above: Operators practising their art; some in training, others for real.

US Forces prepare to storm a suspect's house in central Iraq.

2nd Marine Expeditionary Brigade,
2nd Marine Division
1st, 3rd Battalions, 2nd Marines
2nd Battalion, 8th Marines
1st Battalion, 10th Marines
2nd Amphibious Assault Battalion
2nd Recon Battalion
2nd Light Armored Recon Battalion
2nd, 8th Tank Battalions
15th Marine Expeditionary Unit
24th Marine Expeditionary Unit
26th Marine Expeditionary Unit

AIR FORCE

Special Operations
16th Special Ops Wing (AC-130)
20th Special Ops Squadron (MH-53M)
193rd Special Ops Wing (EC130E)
Ali Al Salem AB, Kuwait
386th Air Exped Group
118th Fighter Squadron (A-10)
41st Electronic Combat Squadron (EC-130)
Al Jaber AB, Kuwait
332nd Air Exped Group
52nd Fighter Wing
22nd, 23rd Fighter Squadrons (F-16)
172nd Fighter Squadron (A-10)
332nd Exped Air Support Ops Squadron
332nd Exped Intelligence Flight
332nd Exped Rescue Squadron (HH-60G)
552nd Air Control Wing (E3 AWACs)
Masirah AB, Oman
355th Air Exped Group
4th Special Ops Squadron (AC-130U)
8th Special Ops Squadron (MC-130E)
Thumrait AB, Oman
405th Air Exped Wing

405th Exped Bomb Wing (B1B)
28th, 34th, 37th Bomb Wings (B1B)
55th Wing (RC-135)
Al Udeid AB, Qatar
379th Air Exped Wing
49th Fighter Wing (F-117)
4th Ops Group (F-15)
336th Fighter Squadron (F-15)
93rd Air Control Wing (E8 J-STARS)
Al Dhafra AB, UAE
380th Air Exped Wing
9th, 57th Recon Wings (U2)
11th, 12th, 15th Recon Squadron (RQ1A)
Prince Sultan AB, Saudi Arabia
363rd Air Exped Wing
14th, 22nd Fighter Squadrons (F-16)
67th, 390th Fighter Squadrons (F-15)
457th, 524th Fighter Squadrons (F-16)
363 Exped Airborne Air Control Squadron (E3 AWACs)
38th Recon Squadron (RC-135)
99th Recon Squadron (U2)
VAQ-142 (EA-6B)

Diego Garcia
40th Air Exped Wing
509th Bomb Wing
20th, 40th Bomb Squadrons (B2)

RAF Fairford, UK
457th Air Exped Group
23rd Bomb Squadron (B52)
509th Bomb Wing
9th Recon Wing

NAVY

Theodore Roosevelt Carrier Battle Group
USS *Theodore Roosevelt* (CVN 71)
Carrier Air Wing 8
USS *Anzi* (CG 68)
USS *Cape St. George* (CG 71)
USS *Arleigh Burke* (DDG 51)
USS *Porter* (DDG 78)
USS *Winston Churchill* (DDG 81)
USS *Stump* (DD 978)
USS *Carr* (FFG 52)
USS *Arctic* (AOE 8)

Harry S. Truman Carrier Battle Group
USS *Harry S. Truman* (CVN 75)

Carrier Air Wing 3
USS *San Jacinto* (CG 56)
USS *Oscar Austin* (DDG 79)
USS *Mitscher* (DDG 57)
USS *Donald Cook* (DDG 75)
USS *Briscoe* (DD 977)
USS *Dey* (DD 989)
USS *Hawes* (FFG 53)
USNS *Kanawha* (T-A196)
USNS *Mount Baker* (T-AE 34)
USS *Pittsburgh* (SSN 720)
USS *Montpelier* (SSN 765)

Kitty Hawk Carrier Battle Group
USS *Kitty Hawk* (CV 63)
Carrier Air Wing 5
USS *Chancellorsville* (CG 62)
USS *Cowpens* (CG 63)
USS *John S. McCain* (DDG 56)
USS *O'Brien* (DD 975)
USS *Cushing* (DD 985)
USS *Vandergrift* (FFG 48)
USS *Gary* (FFG 51)
USS *Bremerton* (SSN 698)

Abraham Lincoln Carrier Battle Group
USS *Abraham Lincoln* (CVN 72)
Carrier Air Wing 14
USS *Mobile Bay* (CG 53)
USS *Shiloh* (CG 67)
USS *Paul Hamilton* (DDG 60)
USS *Fletcher* (DD 992)
USS *Crommlein* (FFG 37)
USS *Reuben James* (FFG 57)
USS *Camden* (AOE 2)
USS *Honolulu* (SSN 718)
USS *Cheyenne* (SSN 773)

Constellation Carrier Battle Group
USS *Constellation* (CV 64)
Carrier Air Wing 2
USS *Valley Forge* (CG 50)
USS *Bunker Hill* (CG 52)
USS *Higgins* (DDG 76)
USS *Thach* (FFG 43)
USS *Ranier* (AOE 7)
USS *Columbia* (SSN 771)
USS *Milius* (DDG 69)

Nimitz Carrier Battle Group
USS *Nimitz* (CVN 68)
Carrier Air Wing 11
USS *Princeton* (CG 59)
USS *Chosin* (CG 65)
USS *Fitzgerald* (DDG 62)
USS *Benfold* (DDG 65)
USS *Oldendorf* (DD 972)
USS *Rodney M. Davis* (FFG 60)
USS *Pasadena* (SSN 752)
USS *Bridge* (AOE-10)

Amphibious Task Force East
USS *Saipan* (LHA 2)
USS *Gunston Hall* (LSD 44)
USS *Ponce* (LPD 15)
USS *Bataan* (LHD 5)
USS *Kearsage* (LHD 3)

USS *Ashland* (LSD 48)
USS *Portland* (LSD 37)
Marine Aircraft Group 29

Amphibious Task Force West
USS *Boxer* (LHD 4)
USS *Bonhomme Richard* (LHD 6)
USS *Cleveland* (LPD 7)
USS *Dubuque* (LPD 8)
USS *Anchorage* (LSD 36)
USS *Comstock* (LSD 45)
USS *Pearl Harbor* (LSD 52)

Tarawa Amphibious Ready Group
USS *Tarawa* (LHA 1)
USS *Duluth* (LPD 6)
USS *Rushmore* (LSD 47)
Nassau Amphibious Ready Group
USS *Nassau* (LHA 4)
USS *Austin* (LPD 4)
USS *Tortuga* (LSD 46)

Iwo Jima Amphibious Ready Group
USS *Iwo Jima* (LHD 7)
USS *Nashville* (LPD 13)
USS *Carter Hall* (LSD 50)

Mine Countermeasures Div 31
USS *Ardent* (MCM 12)
USS *Dextrous* (MCM 13)
USS *Cardinal* (MHC 60)
USS *Raven* (MHC 61)

Above: A USAF CSAR helicopter deploys for a destination unknown at the height of Operation Iraqi Freedom.

The Nighthawk - perfect for precision strike and decapitation missions - hence its use in attacks on Iraqi targets.

CHAPTER EIGHT

CONCLUSION

As I write this final page, chaos is reigning supreme in Iraq as there are still those who mourn Saddam's demise. Although their numbers may be small in relation to the size of the country, they are still sizeable enough to cause our military forces problems. And as history has shown time and time again, the only way to beat subversives or terrorists is to fight them at their own game. Only Special Forces can do that.

During Operation Iraqi Freedom, some 10,000 US Special Forces personnel were deployed for combat operations, hence the quick defeat of Saddam's conventional military forces. But for us to win the peace we must commit even more Special Forces to the region, as only they can bring about the defeat of the unconventional Iraqi forces that now prevail there. And defeat them they must, for the consequences of failure do not bear thinking about, as the genie of insurrection is an evil beast that will grow and grow until it consumes all in its path.

Special Forces are not supermen, nor indeed are they Gods. They are common soldiers, who soldier uncommonly well and we are blessed to have such people protecting us.

ABBREVIATIONS

AAA	Anti-Aircraft Artillery	HALO	High Altitude Low Opening
AAB	Air Assault Brigade	IR	Infrared
ABG	Armoured Battle Group	ISA	Intelligence Support Activity
ADV	Air Defence Variant	JCS	Joint Chiefs of Staff
AFSOC	Air Force Special Operations	JHC	Joint Helicopter Command
AFV	Armoured Fighting Vehicle	JSTARS	Joint Surveillance and Target Radar System
APC	Armoured Personnel Carrier	KSK	Kommando Spezialkrafte
AWACS	Airborne Warning and Control System	LCAC	Landing Craft Air Cushion
		LPH	Landing Platform Helicopter
BDA	Battle Damage Assessment	LRDG	Long Range Desert Group
BRF	Brigade Reconnaissance Force	LSV	Light Strike Vehicle
C2	Command and Control	MBT	Main Battle Tank
C4I	Command, Control, Communications, Computers and Intelligence	MLRS	Multiple Launch Rocket System
		MOD	Ministry of Defence
		NATO	North Atlantic Treaty Organization
CAP	Combat Air Patrol		
CAS	Close Air Support	SAR	Synthetic Aperture Radar
CALCM	Conventionally Armed Air Launched Cruise Missiles	SAS	Special Air Service
		SAM	Surface-to Air-Missile
CIA	Central Intelligence Agency	SBS	Special Boat Service
COG	Centre Of Gravity	SEAD	Suppression Enemy Air Defences
CRW	Counter Revolutionary Warfare	SF	Special Forces
CSAR	Combat Search and Rescue	SOCOM	Special Operations Command
CV(F)	Carrier Vessel Fleet	SOG	Special Operations Group
DoD	Department of Defense	STOVL	Short Take-Off and Vertical Landing
E & E	Escape and Evasion		
EOD	Explosive ordnance disposal	TACBE	Tactical Beacon
		UAV	Unmanned Air Vehicle
FBI	Federal Bureau of Investigation	UCAV	Unmanned Combat Air Vehicle
FCS	Future Combat System	UN	United Nations
GPS	Global Positioning System	WMD	Weapons Mass Destruction
HAHO	High Altitude High Opening		

INDEX

BAGHDAD or BUST

THE INSIDE STORY OF GULF WAR 2

MIKE RYAN

Here for the first time is revealed the true and compelling story of the sensationally successful joint US and UK campaign to liberate Iraq from the oppressive regime of Saddam Hussein from its conception to dramatic conclusion.

The author uses his unique knowledge and network of contacts to describe the meticulous planning of this massive undertaking, which involved the mustering of land, sea and air forces from thousands of miles away. He examines the logistical and political problems that at times appeared insurmountable and the nail-biting tensions and manoeuvring behind the scenes conducted under conditions of extreme pressure and secrecy.

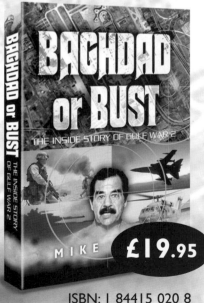

The graphic account of the military operations once hostilities began in such dramatic fashion makes for riveting reading drawing as they do on the experiences of those who fought in the frontline and in the air. The book also delves into those curses of modern warfare, friendly fire incidents and collateral damage, and why, even with all the marvels of modern technology, we still cannot prevent tragedies happening.

With its powerful selection of images and highly informed narrative *Baghdad or Bust* makes for compelling reading.

Superbly illustrated • Printed in full colour • Hardback
For further details, contact us now on:

01226 734555

£19.95

ISBN: 1 84415 020 8

E-mail:**sales@pen-and-sword.co.uk**
Website:**www.pen-and-sword.co.uk**

PEN & SWORD MILITARY BOOKS